Understanding & Training
Puppies

Understanding & Training
Puppies

Barbara Sykes

The Crowood Press

First published in 2002 by
The Crowood Press Ltd
Ramsbury, Marlborough
Wiltshire SN8 2HR

www.crowood.com

This impression 2012

British Library Cataloguing-in-Publication Data
A catalogue record for this book is available from the British
Library.

ISBN 978 1 86126 522 7

Dedication
I would like to dedicate this book to Malcolm and Maureen in appre-
ciation of all their hard work and patience and their friendship.

Acknowledgements
Photographs by Malcolm and Maureen Merone, Madeleine Hacking
and the author.

Typeset by Phoenix Typesetting, Burley-in-Wharfedale, West Yorkshire

Printed and bound in India by Replika Press Pvt. Ltd.

CONTENTS

INTRODUCTION

It is a big responsibility looking after and bringing up a puppy. His education, good manners and social behaviour will be dependent on your ability to be a good pack leader. His self-confidence will either blossom or wilt according to how you treat him, and your ability to be a strong pack leader. Learning to be a pack leader is an accepted part of dog training but unfortunately it is often interpreted to fit human behaviour rather than canine. For example a theory that demands you ignore your dog if it misbehaves is a human theory, as the pack will not ignore misdemeanours, they will educate. Your dog walking with its head in front of your leg is a human theory, as no pack leader allows the pack to walk in front.

In this book we are not concentrating on training, in fact I am a big believer in allowing a puppy to mature in its own time and being able to enjoy its puppyhood. Training is for extra activities and should not be confused with good manners and good behaviour. A puppy who can fetch a ball and distinguish one toy from another may be clever but if it ignores you and will not come back when it is called it is bad mannered and will not be a pleasure to take on a walk. Four clear, non-negotiable instructions explained to your puppy as soon as possible will instate you as a pack leader in his eyes.

Puppies of all breeds are born with certain instincts, and their mother will not only have nurtured these instincts, she will also have begun early education. The following pages are to help you to understand what these instincts are and what your puppy will expect from you.

By recognizing his canine instincts you can use them to help you to teach him how to behave in your home and to explain to him that you are his pack leader. If your puppy does not perceive you as his pack leader he will be like a child without parental guidance, the result of which can be manifest in nervousness, aggression or just unruly bad manners.

The following pages are designed to help you to see the world through your puppy's eyes, to learn to communicate with him in a language he understands and to know instinctively what he needs. *To learn to think dog.*

CHAPTER 1

CREATING A PICTURE

Talk to anyone who has reared a puppy and most will say 'they are only a puppy for a very short time'. This is so true, and although some breeds may develop physically before others, the actual puppy stage, the sweet cuddly little bundle of fun that appeals to everyone, lasts but a few short weeks. If the puppy stage was over so quickly it would seem that a book on puppy management would only be a few short pages: after all, what is there to learn about, other than feeding and basic training? If that were true there would be many more better behaved adult dogs, far fewer problem dogs and fewer dogs in rescue centres.

Looking after and rearing a puppy begins before it enters your house, in some cases before it is born, and every part of its early education is the assembly of a foundation of good manners for its future. Consider each day of a puppy's life as a piece of a jigsaw, which if correctly selected and placed will shape a wonderful picture that can bring years of happiness; but remember it will be difficult to create a perfect picture if pieces are damaged or misplaced. So we are not just talking about the first few weeks of a puppy's life, we are looking at all the pieces of the jigsaw and fitting them together in a way that can create an individual picture of each puppy and owner. To do this we need to look at how the picture can look if it has flaws so we will keep diversifying from puppyhood

to the mature dog with a problem. In so doing we will see how a small, simple mistake made at puppyhood can create a large and not-so-simple-to-solve problem a few months later.

How can puppy management begin before you get a puppy? Because when the puppy comes into your home on that very first day you need to have a 'game plan'. You need to have a bed and a 'safe area' for it, you need a set of rules and you must be clear in your own mind what they are for, because a puppy will not understand you changing them. You need to have done sufficient research to know that you have chosen the right breed for you and your way of life. Also that what you have decided on, whether a pedigree, a cross breed or a rescue, was your decision and not one influenced by other members of your family, or well-meaning friends. In short, you need to give a lot of time and thought to your reasons for wanting a puppy, what breed and where to get it, and then be prepared to spend even more time helping it mature into a sensible adult dog.

Puppies are wonderful to watch, they are cuddly and they are fun to be with, but they grow very quickly into smart adolescents who will try to outwit their owners at every turn if they have not been taught to respect them. I have lost track of the number of times I have heard a distraught owner of a wayward adolescent dog tell me they had not begun to train their puppy until it was four or five months old. In other words it had lost its cute 'butter wouldn't melt in its mouth' appeal and was becoming a problem. But what to the owner is a problem, to the puppy has become a way of life. If it has never been taught anything other than what it is doing, and if this was acceptable behaviour to the owner when it was a puppy, the owner cannot now suddenly change the rules by deciding it is no longer acceptable and expect the puppy to understand this. For example if a puppy has been given toys and has chewed them, it may not seem to pose a problem. But when it is an adolescent and has progressed to 'bigger and better' things to chew, such as chair legs and skirting

Puppies are irresistible but they soon grow up. Make sure you know how big your puppy will be when he is an adult.

boards, where are the rules that say 'you do not chew in my house?' The owner may then decide to impose new rules, but to the dog it is only doing what it has been led to believe is acceptable.

When I point this out to people I often receive the answer, 'Well, it was only a puppy, it was too young to understand and I wanted it to enjoy its puppyhood'. So at what point *was* the erring young-ster expected to suddenly be able to understand, and what kind of a youth is in store for it if it is constantly being told it is badly behaved, albeit because it has not been taught any better? It is important to make the rules clear from the start, which is all part of parenting, and which in turn produces a strong and dependable leader.

Why Parenting?

Few things in life are truly unique and most things have a parallel, for example taking a dog into your home is similar to taking in a foster child. Communicating with a dog for the first time is similar to communicating with another human being who does not speak your language. Being in control of a dog is similar to being a canine pack leader, and bringing up a puppy is similar to bringing up children. Parents make sure their children are well mannered and have a grasp of most everyday scenarios before they go to school. Parents provide a safe haven for their children, they encourage them to come to them in times of trouble and they protect them, whilst at the same time

It is never easy choosing a puppy but make sure you select from a healthy litter. These puppies are all in good condition and are all similar in size.

encouraging them to be individuals. Pack leaders protect their pack, they offer security and a strong dependable leadership, and there is a great similarity between the pack leader educating the pack and the parent educating the child.

If we look at sensible parenting, good manners will be one of the first essentials to be taught to a child. Parents will not wait until the child is reaching adolescence and is constantly pushing people over to gain access to the door, or has destroyed the garden or house due to sheer lack of respect. Children are taught good manners as a matter of course, and sensible parenting will allow a child to develop both character and confidence within the confines of the home environment as preparation for the adult world. The role of the puppy owner is to make sure their puppy grows up to respect them as a pack leader, to teach it good manners, and to allow it to develop character and confidence within the pack (home) environment. The role of parent, pack leader and puppy owner are all united in the fact that they provide guidelines, security, rules, confidence and mental stimulation.

Quite often the owner of a new puppy will be tempted to ignore certain behaviour, deeming it to be part of puppy development and something the youngster will eventually grow out of. But if a child were to be bad mannered, would that be considered part of natural development? Would the parents expect the child to grow out of it, or would parental tuition embrace the education of good manners at a very early age in order to prevent misunderstandings as the child matures? If we compare the development of the puppy and the child we can see the comparisons, the need for guidelines and the importance of good manners.

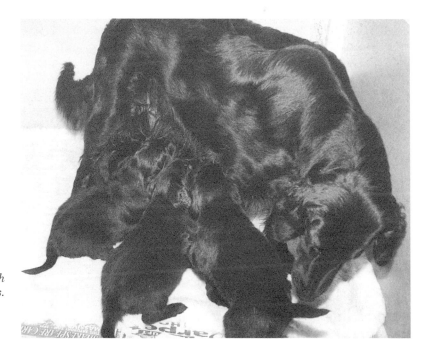

A bitch in good condition will feel well, will enjoy looking after her pups, and will teach them good manners.

Advantages

How can anyone resist a puppy? They are wonderful, and in the words of a shepherd watching his lambs frolicking in the field, 'It's a grand relaxing job watching them, proper little time wasters they are . . .'. Anything young is a joy to watch, the antics they get up to, the learning process, the wonder of newness in everything they see, taste and experience. In fact we can almost relive some of our own first discoveries and fears; we do it with our children, and in many instances puppies will receive similar attention from humans as babies will from adults.

The whole world will suddenly want to know you when you have a puppy in your arms. Neighbours, friends and relatives will visit, and all will want a cuddle. For a while you and your household will be in demand, and there will be no shortage of 'puppy sitters' if you have to go somewhere and leave it on its own for a while. You can have hours of fun playing with it, and there is no shortage of 'toys' in the pet shops for you to fill his bed with and boast an overflowing toy box.

When buying a puppy, get to know all about his background, enquire about his ancestors and if they are a reliable breed line, his breeders and if they are reliable, sensible breeders. This information will give you a head start in educating him, as you will then know which genetic traits to enhance and which to keep in the background. This puppy comes to you as a blank book and it is up to you to fill in the pages. The well mannered adult dog you have dreamed of, and who will be a joy to be with, is there in that little bundle, and all you have to do is bring it up correctly. You can begin to guide your dog's education down whatever path you may wish to follow. No dog is perfect but your pitfalls should be minimal, as you are the one feeding the information necessary to your puppy in order for it to mature into a sensible intelligent adult dog.

Disadvantages

Allow me to finish the shepherd's quote from the previous page '. . . but when they grow out of being happy work they become hard work!' In fact we can almost rewrite the last section: 'It may be a joy to watch a puppy's antics but you will need to be able to differentiate between harmless fun and something that will almost certainly develop into first, a bad habit and eventually a behavioural problem.' We do often talk to and treat puppies like babies but they are *not* human babies, they are young dogs, and as they mature their canine instincts will develop, and no amount of baby talk will convince your dog that you are a pack leader if you have not developed a canine communication link with him.

It may seem wonderful that everyone wants to come and admire your new puppy, but all that attention can often do more harm than good. The puppy sitters may not be as keen to oblige when the cute stage has disappeared and the dog is showing signs of being undisciplined. It will do no harm to leave the puppy on his own for a short while, but it can do plenty of harm to confuse him until he doesn't know who he is supposed to look up to. You may have hours of fun playing games and with lots of toys, but if you do not teach him how to use them correctly you will not have fun trying to DIY the house after he has tried to rearrange it!

The background information for your puppy is only as reliable as the breeder you

Puppies that are used to their own sleeping area will settle quickly in their new home if they are provided with a cage.

are buying from, and the names of the ancestors mean nothing if the temperaments cannot be described to you. Being from winning lines is not as important as being from reliable lines. The well educated dog you have always dreamed of is there for you to mould, but remember, you only have yourself to blame if it all goes wrong!

Your Own Signature

Hopefully the above will not have dissuaded you from having a puppy, but if it has, then you will know in your own heart that it is not the right time at the moment to be introducing a small, dependant, time-consuming being into your life. If you are now going to go ahead and take a puppy into your life, then you know of some of the possible pitfalls ahead. Or maybe you already have a puppy, and now you are feeling that at least so far you have got it right – or are you one of the puppy owners who is already trying to DIY the kitchen cupboard doors? But maybe so far you are just curious and wanting to read a book about puppy management to see if you got it right, or if there are any new ideas in this book that you haven't already read about. Maybe your curiosity will turn into a new training regime, maybe you have had a small problem with your dog that is not of major concern but you could well do without having to put up with. You cannot turn the clock back but, as in all structures, you can take some of the walls down, strengthen the foundation and rebuild a bigger and better building. So if

Senior canines educate puppies in the pack. These two youngsters are being chaperoned by an older cousin.

you have begun to read out of curiosity but have not got a puppy, I can promise you that just as good puppy management will produce a good adult dog, so can a problem adult dog benefit from good puppy management.

No one else can tell you *exactly* what you can or cannot do with your puppy for they are not living with it or training it. However, there are certain rules that you *must* adhere to: you must make sure your dog knows you are the pack leader, you must teach good manners, and you must teach the four golden non-negotiable rules of basic pack behaviour – to stop, wait, come back, and fall into pack position when told to by the pack leader. These rules are mandatory and they go hand in glove, so without any one of them you and your dog will have a breakdown in communication. When correctly applied, these rules will give you a well mannered and respectful dog and you can then choose where to go from there. You can train for any of the disciplines or you can enjoy sharing your life with one of the most loyal companions you may ever meet. But whatever you do with the rest of your time together, you need to develop your own style of training. No matter what you are training for, you need to create and personalize your own style; athletes may compete in the same competition but they will each have developed their own style. A racehorse will have certain things that improve its performance and some that will hamper it; individual training will still provide a horse that gallops, but it may also provide one that wins. Each family lives by the rules of society, but within their own domain they have their own style of living. It is now up to you to create from the blank book of puppyhood a text that follows all the rules of the pack, but is individual to you. You must learn to write your own signature. Only then can your dog grow into a companion that understands you, and only then can you create an empathy with your dog.

Chapter Summary

All puppies are lovable but they grow up very quickly. Leaving the education of a puppy until it is an adolescent dog is like waiting until a child becomes a teenager to teach him good manners. Early education should be tailored to suit your home and lifestyle, but there are certain rules of behaviour all puppies must learn.

CHAPTER 2

NATURAL INSTINCTS

The choosing of a puppy is not to be taken lightly: you are not bringing into your home something that can be exchanged, given away, or returned if it doesn't come up to expectations. You are going to bring a living being into your home that needs caring for – however, feeding, grooming, exercise and games are not enough. If you were to adopt a child you would be interviewed and would have to supply references and fit certain criteria before being passed as suitable adoptive parents. Good parenting does not supply endless free time, toys and games, and the freedom to make decisions; it is about education, good manners, communication, and teaching how to make decisions: you are a parent and mentor. When you take on the responsibility of a puppy you are becoming an adoptive parent and pack leader. Parents teach children, they share quality time with them, play with them and guide them, but their undisputed role is senior, they are not surrogate brothers and sisters. If your role of pack leader is not made clear to your puppy you will become a sibling, a littermate to play and romp with but not commanding the respect of a leader. It may seem harmless when the puppy play fights when it is young, but some of the interaction of adolescent siblings is neither fun nor harmless when

It is important your puppy sees you as a pack leader and not a littermate. When siblings play fight, biting each other is not against the rules.

it incorporates a human being. Puppies will play and use their teeth on each other, adolescents will play fight and test each other's wrestling skills. This kind of play with a human being can result in someone being bitten, but as far as the dog is concerned it will be doing what you have allowed it to do. Parents can be their child's best friend and confidant, but this does not impede the learning process, in fact it will enhance it. So your aim with your puppy is to have controlled fun, to educate it, to protect it, to guide it and to understand it.

Taking a puppy into your home is a big responsibility and one that should not be considered if your daily commitments mean you will be unable to provide the stability, patience and understanding that it will need. However, you do not have to become a slave to its every whim, in fact you will only make life difficult for yourself if you do and your puppy will become demanding. But you need to be firm with yourself, as puppies can be very hard to resist. A puppy can become overtired and it can be demanding, and you will have to learn to know when it is genuinely in need of attention and when it is in need of rest. This will be easier if you have some prior knowledge of the breed of dog you have chosen and of any possible inherited characteristics.

Choosing a Puppy

Most people know what breed of dog they would like, but even so there are a few things that must be taken into consideration. A single person with no family commitments may have plenty of free time available outside working hours. But plenty of time at the end of a working day cannot justify a puppy having to spend all, or even part, of each day on its own. A family of two adults may have a similar problem unless one partner does not work,

This is normal behaviour for two dogs play fighting, but a human being must not be seen by a dog to be a play partner in this kind of game.

This is a wonderful picture of two dogs wrestling in the air. All the balance and the weight is on the back leg of one dog. This is how adult dogs play and no adult should be allowed to play with a young dog in this manner. Once again it is acceptable for dogs to use their teeth as they will not hurt each other, but they could inflict serious injury on a person who tried to play a wrestling game with them.

or works only a few hours a week. Even so, for the first few weeks someone should be available throughout each day. I do not believe that a puppy should be left on its own for a long time, or even for regular shorter periods; however, it is not always practicable nor beneficial for you to be on hand every moment of the day. A puppy needs to learn to be content with its own company, to learn how to keep itself amused, and it should be encouraged to have a 'quiet time'. But this is part of its education, and not a reason to leave it for hours on end in the name of training.

When you have considered all your options you will find that some breeds will be more suitable than others. For example an energetic family who spend a lot of time outdoors may not find a small dog compatible to their lifestyle. Similarly someone who is not inclined towards outdoor activities, or lives in a small house, would not be suited to a dog with an energetic attitude. The size of a dog is relevant to your accommodation, but it does not always dictate the amount of exercise it needs. If it did, a small breed would be presumed to be in need of far less exercise than a very large breed of dog. But some small dogs can be very energetic – terriers were originally bred to work, and although there is a variety of terrier breeds, some of them require plenty of exercise. Many of the medium-sized dogs are working breeds, for example border collies, dalmations, spaniels and GSDs, and these breeds need a great deal of both mental and physical exercise. Some of the larger, heavier breeds of dog will not necessarily need an abundance of exercise, but neither are they suited to small houses or gardens, and quite often some of these breeds have other special requirements; for example, Old English sheepdogs and Newfoundlands require plenty of special attention regarding grooming. So when you are visualizing your puppy you also need to think of the adult dog that it will become, and make sure you have the facilities and time to cater for it when it is no longer small and cute.

Pedigree, cross breed, rescue: more decisions for you to make. A pedigree dog is one whose ancestry can be proven by means of stud records and a breed sheet (family tree); dogs registered with a society specifically for that breed will be a dog with a proven pedigree. A registered dog is registered with a society or club. Dogs registered with the Kennel Club can be pedigree or registered cross breeds. It may sound confusing, but at least you now have the chance to understand it prior to buying a puppy, thus avoiding any possible confusion. For the purpose of breeding or competing in some of the disciplines, registration will be necessary with the Kennel Club. A registered pup with a proven pedigree may also be eligible for registration in the society dedicated to its breed, for example sheepdogs, huskies, Newfoundland. A cross breed is obviously not eligible for registration in a breed society but it is possible for such a dog to fit into a Kennel Club registration category, though this is not for breeding or showing purposes. Rescue societies will have mixed breeds and cross breeds, but if you know what breed you want, then you may have more choice if you look for a rescue establishment dedicated to that particular breed. There are likely to be fewer problems taking on a rescue puppy than an older rescue dog as you will be teaching your own rules and will not have the problems of trying to understand what a previous owner has, or has not, taught.

There should be no pressure on you to make a decision to buy a puppy when you first go to look at a litter, and if the person selling the puppies does try to urge you to make a quick decision it may be worth questioning their motives. A caring breeder should be more concerned about the kind of home the puppy is going to than making a quick sale. However, when you decide that you do want to choose a puppy from a particular litter, don't waste time looking for something you may never find. I knew someone who once spent several hours trying to make up his mind which puppy to have out of a litter he had gone to see. Several years later when the one of his choice failed to come up to expectations he claimed he had chosen the wrong pup! Whichever puppy you choose when you get it home, it will be yours, and whatever happens to it, whether it wins great accolades or simply keeps your feet warm on a night, it will be an important part of your life.

If there is only one puppy available then choosing one is not an option, but if there is a choice, most people will be persuaded either by particular markings or by characteristics. One of the puppies may carry similar markings to a previous dog or it may have a distinctive marking that has an immediate appeal. Some may criticize choosing by markings, but at least this

This little army is on the march with the one at the front choosing where to go and who to see; if he does not take the lead, another puppy will. The one at the back is not necessarily shy, he is just taking his place in the team.

way you are not carrying a preconceived idea of how your puppy should develop. Choosing for certain characteristics can be misleading, for the behaviour seen in the litter can change, or be changed, as the puppy develops. Some people will be convinced their puppy chose them, though on most occasions the puppy was simply investigating. There may be some link when a person looks at a puppy, almost like recognition, and I am the last person to decry this possibility. For when I am choosing a puppy for myself I will make my mind up when it is still very young. It will make no difference if it is marked like a zebra and hides in a corner: if it is the one I feel is mine, then so be it, in fact I will quite often *choose* the one that sits at the back watching.

It is worth remembering that every puppy pack has a leader, and when a stranger is in their midst, this little general will be the one to investigate. If you choose this puppy on the strength that it came to you, which puppy would you have chosen if this one had been out of the equation, maybe being cuddled by someone else? It's a fair assumption that another one would have stepped into its paw marks and rallied forth to find out who you were. I learned years ago that assumptions as to how a puppy can develop can lead to unhappiness. I had a dog brought to me for rehabilitation that had been bought as a puppy by a gentleman who competed in obedience competitions; he ran several clubs and wanted a strong-minded dog. He had chosen from a litter a real robust little guy that became shy and introvert because his owner thought he needed to be kept in his place. But I have also had the pleasure of helping a retired couple to understand their quiet and seemingly shy little puppy, who later became so confident her owners began successfully competing with her. The dog at the front of the litter is quite often the one who is good at making decisions and has a mind of its own, and the one at the back is usually a quieter puppy. But the way you handle your pup, how you educate it, and how good a pack leader you are, should enable you to balance its strengths and weaknesses, thus providing a well balanced, well behaved dog.

Natural Instincts

So what instincts does a puppy have? It will have within it all the instincts it needs to survive, but they will not all be balanced: some will be tipped high on the scales, and some will be below the balance line. It is up to, first the breeder and then the owner, to study the puppy and decide how to nurture certain instincts and how to balance them in order to produce a well bred, well mannered puppy. The breeder's responsibility is to ensure that the breed lines of the parents of the litter are compatible. This means that the breeding of the ancestors must be studied, and strengths and weaknesses must be balanced. If the owner of one or both of the parents is not capable of doing, this then there is every possibility that the litter will not be of balanced temperament. Having bred from compatible lines the breeder must then make sure the puppies are brought up with certain rules and should be sufficiently knowledgeable to be able to advise which puppy is most suited to which potential purchaser. There is no such thing as the perfect line; this is why it is important that the breeder should be knowledgeable about breeding for compatibility of genes rather for looks or certain skills. There are no guarantees when it comes to breeding. Puppies can be born with a heart defect or any other defect, and heartbreaking as it is for the new owner, the breeder can rarely be blamed for a congenital problem, although most breeders will be sensitive to the situation and will help as much as they can. However, the risk of most hereditary problems can and should be minimal with good planned breeding.

When a puppy enters your home you are responsible for its welfare and its education. By building on the foundation the breeder has started, you can direct and control the education of your puppy in the direction you want it to go. But if it destroys your kitchen and chases next door's cat, don't ring the breeder and ask them why, because somewhere along the way you have actually led your puppy to believe that this behaviour is acceptable! Being a well bred dog does not mean it will train itself to understand you and what you want. It is a young dog, and if you don't guide its natural canine instincts as a senior pack member should do, then expect it to behave like any other wayward youngster of any species when good manners have not been made a priority.

In the wild its mother will have given a puppy certain rules during the first few weeks of its life: she will have instructed where and when it can play, eat, foul and sleep. When the puppies are old enough they will graduate to the adolescent pack and the senior canines will teach, guide and educate the youngsters how to become an integral part of the pack. A good breeder will allow natural development for the litter, permitting mum to prepare her offspring for life after weaning. Always look to the natural pack development for guidance on management, for the pack are the original script writers, not humans. When your puppy enters your home it will expect to see a pack leader, a senior canine, to carry on the tuition and guidance its mother has already begun.

She will have taught it to walk behind her unless given permission to do otherwise. For all those who have been given to understand that changing direction will make your dog recall, or walk to heel, I can assure you this method is for puppies, it is used by the mother, and rarely more than once. If the puppy does not heed her first time she will be justifiably annoyed with it, for to ignore mum can be a security risk for the pack. It will know where it can foul,

When mum teaches her offspring good manners they will be happy to give the same respect to a human being. These littermates feel secure when they are behind their human pack leader and they will happily follow behind when he or she moves.

and it will understand which part of the pack area it can play in and which part is for resting. It will also have been provided with a safe place to sleep, one safe from intruders, and it will have begun to play survival games. These games are designed to encourage puppies to find their strongest survival instinct and to nurture it. When the puppy pack graduates, each will have a 'strongest' instinct, and when the puppies play more advanced survival games they will begin to form a strong team working as one unit, each one being a specialist at what it is naturally best at. But having a strong instinct does not mean the other instincts are not there, it simply means they tip their strongest instinct high on the scales of balance; but should one of the team drop out, then other instincts would immediately come up to balance what had been lost.

Puppies are taught by mum to follow and not to go in front without permission. This little chap knows to give the same respect to grandma.

Recognizing Natural Instincts

The breeder should be able to tell you about your puppy's strongest instincts. However, if you watch the litter interacting with each other you will be able to see which puppy likes to use its teeth, which play fights on top, which is usually underneath, which appears to be the thinker, and so on. But remember, they each develop instincts to provide a whole unit, so when the one who likes to use its teeth is removed, another one will tip that same instinct a little higher on the scales of balance to compensate. Now remember that the 'whole' they are creating is for survival, and they will go into the senior pack and take their places as a valuable part of a hunting team. The only difference in the breeds is the way they hunt and kill to survive; for example, senior members will educate terriers how to locate and expose underground prey, and larger breeds will be taught how to outwit bigger and faster larger prey.

These puppies will learn by playing, but every game is for a reason and must be played correctly; there can be no room for mistakes. For example when interacting they will appear to be playing a game of tag, they will run and twist and turn, but they will not chase each other mindlessly around, and if they were to do so the senior pack would reprimand them. It is far harder to catch prey with mindless chasing than it is to outwit it! When puppies tug at a stick they are learning how to use their teeth for survival, and they will ultimately learn how to kill. Now transfer this knowledge to the seemingly harmless games of tuggy played by humans with a puppy. They are encouraging the puppy to tip this instinct high on the scales of balance, and if the

Butter wouldn't melt in his mouth, would it? But he will soon be a boisterous adolescent and if he has not learnt how to behave when he is young he will be a handful in a few short months.

puppy already has this instinct naturally high, then the chances are it will become destructive, and later maybe even aggressive. But when this appears to humans to be a dog with a problem, it is actually a dog responding to other pack members and doing what it has been allowed and encouraged to do.

Games of pack development are overseen by senior members who will join in to teach and to guide; but most of the time they allow the youngsters to develop their own style within the pack rules of hunting. Humans tend to dictate to a dog how to play, for example they expect a dog to 'fetch' a ball. Why? This is a human game, and if a dog is left to its own devices it can quite often develop a far more interesting and fun game than repeatedly bringing back the same object for its owner to throw away again! Toys are for humans; dogs are quite capable of finding something to amuse themselves, and they are also capable of sitting quietly within the pack area and being peaceful. Transfer this pack knowledge to the domestic dog, who is often not only encouraged to play, chase and chew, but is allowed to do it in the home, the pack area, and you can begin to understand why a young dog is always on the go and only rests when it is worn out. It has never been taught to switch off, instead it has been encouraged to commit itself to always running around and looking for entertainment instead of being content with its own company once in a while. The 'quiet area' at school was an accepted way of winding down excited children, and children will not be allowed to kick footballs and play other accepted outdoor sports in the home.

This does not mean to say that human games are not acceptable for dogs, but it is important for a dog to understand its place in the pack. If a human is going to play-fight and wrestle with a dog, then there is a great danger of that dog seeing the human being as a littermate. If this happens then the dog will assume the role of leader of the litter. Similarly if a child plays with a dog and the dog is not taught to respect the child, then their roles are in danger of being littermates, and litter-mates bite each other. You must become the pack leader, and until your puppy sees you as being the one in control, then any interaction that can lead the puppy to perceive you as littermate or equal pack member must be avoided.

I can promise you that it can be as much, or more, fun learning to play the game of pack leader and of playing creative games rather than robust ones. And you can derive even more fun from learning how to use the dog's instincts to create a natural communication between you.

It's now time to look at a puppy's natural instincts in relation to house rules.

Chapter Summary

When choosing a puppy, take into consideration the size and temperament of the breed of your choice when it is mature, and don't be tempted to buy a puppy because it appeared to choose you. Usually this is the puppy pack leader being inquisitive.

Puppies will balance each other's natural instincts when interacting with each other, and all their games will be educational.

If you do not keep the natural instincts balanced when you are training your puppy you can inadvertently cause problems that can sometimes lead to aggression.

The puppy's mother will have taught it good manners and pack behaviour, which provides a foundation for you to build on if you use its natural instincts to educate it.

CHAPTER 3

EARLY LEARNING

After you have decided what breed of puppy you want, have found the litter you want to choose from and have made your final choice of puppy, you are on your own. So that you make as few mistakes as possible (and making mistakes is inevitable – it's how you rectify them that matters) it is important that on the first day you bring your puppy home you ensure he has a secure and recognizable environment. This does not necessarily mean providing the identical bed and surroundings that the breeder provided, although some recognition in this department helps; however, you do need to supply your puppy with information that

his instincts will recognize. If you make a mistake in trying to emulate exactly what the breeder provided, the puppy will not understand you, but if you come even fairly close to natural provision, then the puppy's instinct will help it to understand you.

Knowledge of what the puppy would expect comes from understanding what the pack would provide. We already know that mum would provide a safe and secure sleeping area, so this is where you need to start. You can provide a sleeping area in any corner that can be kept free from intruders, but I would strongly recommend a secure, movable pen, and there are

A puppy needs its own bed and one that will make it feel secure; a cage is ideal as it is easy to keep clean and can be used in the car. This dog is happy in his cage, and if the door is shut he will ask for it to be opened so he can go to bed.

plenty to choose from. Portable cages are probably the most popular as they are collapsible, but they do leave the puppy exposed unless you cover the cage with a blanket. Plastic carrying cages, export type, are to be recommended for privacy, but they are not as easy to dismantle. If you are handy at DIY you can make a secure box with a door, but wooden boxes are not as easy to keep clean. This is your puppy's bed, its 'safe area', and it needs to be placed where it can rest undisturbed and where it can be safe in the knowledge that no strangers will invade its privacy.

There are several reasons for advising a closed-in bed, but I must stress that it must be a place of peace and safety, and *not* a place to shut a puppy away for hours at a time; the idea is for the puppy to have its own 'home' within your pack area. Consider a tribe of Indians: the big chief is the leader, the decision-maker, and providing the tribe members respect him and are loyal to him they can lead their own lives within their tepees without him interfering. You are the decision-maker and your puppy is one of your 'clan', but you are entitled to your privacy and he to his.

Having selected the type of cage or bed for your puppy, choose a quiet place in which to situate it. In the middle of a busy kitchen or hallway will not provide the puppy with privacy or peace, neither will he find it easy to rest or wind down if people are constantly walking past him or talking to him. Remember you are parenting, and young children need some-where of their own or somewhere quiet to sleep or simply to rest! There is nothing to prevent you from moving the cage around. It can be in the room during the day when you want to encourage your puppy to sit and be quiet while you are busy, but in the night or if you have a house full of guests the cage should be put in an area where your youngster will not be disturbed. The beauty of a cage or similar is that you can take it with you when you go away, you can put it in the car, or you can move it into a different room and your dog will always recognize it as its own home. Another tip is always to have the same type of sleeping blanket in the cage, then as the puppy matures you can put the blanket down anywhere in the house without moving the cage and your puppy will see it as his bed.

Now you have the sleeping arrange-

If you supply a blanket or quilt in the cage your dog will grow up to regard this as his 'area' and it can easily be moved from room to room.

ments settled, you do not have to purchase anything else apart from food dishes, collar and lead, and food. If you wish to invest in 'toys' select carefully and wisely, and vow not to use them until your puppy knows how to respect them.

If you teach your puppy all the things he expects to be taught in the first few days you will have few problems with him. But if you think it doesn't matter about education until he is a little older or is 'settled in', then you may find you are making a rod for your own back. Your puppy will not be thinking that you are allowing discrepancies in his behaviour until he feels 'at home': he sees it as it is. So if you allow him on the furniture on day one, then why on earth can't he get on the furniture on day two? If you allow him to chew a slipper or something that looks like a slipper, then why can't he always chew slippers? You must begin to 'think dog' – you are a senior canine now, and must give your young charge rules he understands in a language he understands.

First Rules

It will be an exciting day when you first take your puppy home, but remember that although you know what lies ahead, he doesn't; you know where he is going to sleep and what the next few weeks are going to be like for him, but he knows nothing: he has lost his mum and his littermates, he is on his own, all he has to rely on is you, and he doesn't know you. As regards communication, you both speak different languages: his is instinct, body language and limited vocal sounds, yours is all vocal and stilted human body movements that will mean little to him. You may make sounds that soothe him and he may cuddle up to you for security, but if he is not given information and guidelines he can relate to, he will soon begin to form his own rules.

The first things he needs to know are what any other new resident in your home would expect to be told, namely where to sleep, eat, relieve himself and relax; but of

Your puppy must respect your home and must not assume he has free access to it. By asking him to wait for a second in his cage before giving him permission to enter your space you are establishing yourself as above him in the pack hierarchy.

course you cannot tell him all this in your language. Therefore when he is asleep, lay him gently in his cage and close the door, and on this first occasion be sure you are there when he wakes up. Do not make the mistake of letting him come straight out of the cage and allowing him to investigate; if you do this he will soon regard the cage as a temporary bed, the cage door as freedom, and the rest of the house as his own personal space. Open the door, put your hand gently under his chin and ask him to wait for a few seconds, then allow him out; but make sure he sits and says hello to you before he is allowed his freedom. Do this every time for the first day, and your puppy will soon expect to wait to be invited from his bed into your personal space; he will also associate his freedom to leave his bed with you, and not with the cage door opening.

Your puppy's life needs to be divided into two areas: black you cannot do, and white you can do. Leaving the cage without giving you respect is black, waiting to be invited out is white, and the sooner black and white are understood, the sooner your puppy can live in the grey area. If we teach a child not to take the last biscuit from a plate in his formative years as part of good manners, this rule is not to be broken. But as the child matures, he will know when there are more biscuits in the tin or when the last biscuit is there because no one else wants it. The child learns to live in the grey area, so he knows when it is bad mannered to change television channels, and learns that when no one else is watching the current programme he can therefore change channels, because he is in the grey area. The simple fact that the child has been taught black and white means that should he lapse into bad manners on any occasion it

will not be difficult to explain that this is not acceptable. He is of course already aware of this, and is probably testing the boundaries of parental guidance. Of course the set of rules you would give a puppy will be different from those you would give a child, but the main difference is the language barrier. You can explain vocally to a child what you expect, and should you decide to change the rules you can also explain this to a child. However, to begin with you do not have a communal vocal language with your puppy, and once he understands the rules, to change them will throw him into confusion.

You can now see clearly that you must begin as you mean to go on, and you must make sure that your dog understands what you are trying to say to it. Both you and your puppy may love each other to bits but you chose him, he did not knock on your door and ask to be a part of your family and to be included in all activities, neither does he give a fig about your language. He doesn't need to know it, he has his own, and although you may see him as a four-legged puppy and your pet, he is not seeing you as a two-legged human whose language he must understand: to him you are a two-legged dog, and if he doesn't understand your rules he will make his own! One of you must make the effort, and as he already knows what to expect and will write his own script if you don't provide one, then it is up to you to make the effort to understand his language and to communicate with him in a way he understands.

To seek permission to enter your pack area is something a puppy would expect, within the pack, and the method just described of making your puppy wait a couple of seconds before leaving his cage, and of giving you respect for allowing him to do so, explains more than one thing to him. It tells him that you own the area outside the cage, that he must respect that area and not take it for granted, and that because it is your area, you must be hierarchy to him. Simple, isn't it – but that little bit of effort can save so much frustration later, and it makes it clear to the puppy where he stands in the scheme of things. I am not even going to try and convince you that this will eliminate the possibility of any future problems, but it is the start of a good foundation: 'The cage is yours, and the house is mine, and if you don't respect it then you will retire to your cage to think about it.' The cage is not a punishment place it is a safe area, and dogs understand thinking time because senior pack members make sure they spend time reflecting; they are not allowed to charge around all day being demanding.

Now we have an understanding of the cage and its role, we can look at other rules. Your puppy will need something to chew. This is a natural part of development, but if you allow him to chew a selection of things and you allow this in your home, you may find he extends his 'chewy selection' to such wonderfully tasty things as socks, shoes, towels and eventually maybe a kitchen unit or two! Well, why not? If he has squeaky toys, toys with bells, balls and other goodies, and he is allowed to chew them, why can't he chew other things he picks up, other things that he feels must belong to him because there is such a selection – what is the difference between a soft toy and a sock, a chewy and a piece of wood? Puppies in the pack graduate from puppy 'killing' to adolescent 'killing' so he is simply broadening his horizons because you have not made it clear to him that it is not necessary for him to extend his killing knowledge, in fact he doesn't need it at all.

So select *one* thing for him to chew, and if it is not a bone, make sure it is not a replica of something he may find in your house. An old slipper or chewy resemblance of a slipper may seem harmless, but when he graduates to the real thing you cannot justifiably tell him off. Let us

Providing your puppy with something to chew or a toy is fine, but he must not be allowed to chew anything in your home, he must keep it in his cage.

assume you have provided him with a bone; the next rule is that he is allowed to chew this in his cage, but not outside it. If he brings it out to chew, tell him 'no' and put the bone back in the cage. So he now has a choice: he can remain in the cage and enjoy the bone, or he can save the bone until later and come out of the cage. This is a clear black and white rule: 'You can only chew this, and you only chew it in your own area.' Therefore when your puppy picks up something else to chew, take it from him with a 'no', and give him his bone in his cage. Once this rule is understood you will have made it clear that nothing in your house is to be chewed. Let us look at this another way. If you put a child in a room and give him crayons you cannot justifiably be annoyed if he draws on the wallpaper, neither can you be annoyed if you provide paper with the crayons but no rules. If, on the other hand, you provide crayons and paper and then explain where to draw and where not to draw, and if you make sure these rules are understood, then, and only then, could you be forgiven for being upset if the walls are redecorated! Now look at how important it is to explain to your puppy that he is not allowed to chew in your area. As he matures he will of course move into the grey area where he can be given permission to chew a bone outside his cage.

If you are going to supply toys, remember that you should be the focal point of his attention: you are the one on whom he should be depending for information and communication. Be careful you do not become an instrument for him to use with his toys. I always ask owners who come to me for a consultation with a problem adolescent dog how they brought the puppy up, and the answer is usually predictable: lots of toys, chewies, tuggy toys, balls and titbits. The problems are usually just as predictable: failure to respect the owner, short attention span, destruction, no recall, and pulling on a lead. These problems are quite often exacerbated by a diet that is not suited to the breed or the exercise level of the dog.

It is in everyone's best interest that your puppy grows up into a well mannered adult dog. Strangers do not want to be subjected to your dog growling or jumping up at them, neither will they appreciate being mugged in the park as your dog pinches their ball. Friends may love your dog, but they should not be subjected to the third degree because you cannot make your dog behave. You should be able to take your dog anywhere without worrying about his behaviour. A puppy pulling on its lead may not seem a problem, but there is little fun in taking a dog for a walk when you are reduced to impersonating a sled driver! Whether your dog is small or large, it should respect you; after all, you are the one paying the bills. If a small dog pulls on a lead it may not pose the same problem as a large dog, but only because of its stature and strength, or rather lack of it: it is still showing you disrespect, and as such is exhibiting bad manners.

Your Puppy's Toilet Area

You puppy will have been used to whatever bedding and toilet facilities the breeder provided. Although I am a big believer in trying to make sure the puppy has as little disturbance as possible from the normality it has been used to before it comes to you, if you are going to change things, then it should be on the first day in your home. Whatever happens on day one is what your puppy will expect as standard procedure. The breeder will have had a litter to look after and they will probably have been in a kennel, building, whelping pen or large cage. Whatever the facilities, you will be extremely lucky if they have had them loose in the house and have toilet trained them. Many breeders use paper, but I always like to look at things through the dog's eyes and if newspaper on the floor is to be used for a toilet, then why cannot the newspaper on the settee be used as one? No matter how scrupulously clean you are, you rarely completely eradicate the smell from the floor under the paper, and even if your own puppy is weaned from using this area, visiting dogs will find it a delight to use. I am a big believer in using something they will not be able to find elsewhere in the house (there will always be a newspaper somewhere to trigger off a memory of 'I can do this here'), and something they will find readily available outside. I also use a litter tray to avoid leaving tempting smells on the floor.

Be careful of choosing something that is not found easily outside your gate. Sand in a litter tray is a good idea, and a 'garden toilet' can then be made; though you may find your dog will have a problem when you take it away from home if it cannot find any sand. Soil or turf are good litter bases as they can readily be found elsewhere, and there is little to cause confusion when your puppy is outside in the garden; also, when the litter tray is finally discarded there will be no soil to be found in the home. Gravel is something I rarely advise as puppies are rather prone to picking up small stones and gravel when you are not looking, which can be dangerous if they cause a blockage.

No matter what method you choose, you can rest assured that there will be a time when your little treasure will get the better of you, and dogs seem to be masters at waiting for the ideal opportunity. I can remember being very pleased with myself the first time I used a soil litter tray because within a very short time my puppy understood what was required and had no little 'accidents'. However, the well aimed little pile he left me on the soil at the base of my Yuka plant when he was

These puppies are cosy on their bed, but they have been used to using paper for their toilet. Paper is excellent for a litter of puppies as it soaks up the moisture, but when you take your puppy home it may be advisable to use something different and something that he can identify with outside.

nine months old was, I believe, the beginning of the wonderful sense of humour he continued to show for the rest of his life!

It would be foolish to place the litter tray in a position your puppy will not have access to, but remember that you will eventually require him to go outside. Therefore the nearer you can place it to the outside door, the simpler it will be to teach your puppy to go just that bit further. Most puppies will be in need of their toilet area shortly after eating, so watch carefully and learn to 'read' his body language, for the sooner you can understand his actions, the sooner you can teach him what you want. Prevention is better than cure, and if you can take him to where he needs to be

before rather than *after* he has relieved himself, there is less reason for him to misunderstand your requirements. And if your puppy does leave you a puddle, do not make the mistake of panicking: many a puppy has been made hand-shy when their owners have shouted and lunged at them in order to try and prevent what is already inevitable. If you don't see the signs, live with the consequences and vow to do better next time; if not, you may find that when your puppy feels it needs the toilet, it relieves itself where it is through sheer panic at the thought of you being annoyed with it.

You have some good foundation rules now: you have made it clear to your puppy

This cute little line-up are summer babies and are used to being outside during the day. They will not be difficult to house train when they go to their new homes and would benefit from a litter tray with soil in it, as this is what they are used to using.

where he can sleep, and you have made this into a safe and protective area for him. He knows where he can go to relieve himself, and if you have been watching him carefully and have given him regular trips out to the garden he will soon be a clean little chap. He knows that he can only chew inside his cage, and he knows what he is, and is not, allowed to chew. These simple rules will already be giving him the message that you are in a position of authority – but these on their own are not enough to totally convince him that you are the pack leader. You may have many things you want to train him to do, but basically he needs to be well mannered inside and outside your home, and he needs to be well behaved. Good manners are essential, and all you need for a well behaved dog are four commands: stop, stay, walk behind, and the recall. Yes, that's all, but they are non-negotiable, and the best way to teach them is by having fun; but you do not need any balls, toys or titbits. All you need apart from your puppy is you. So now that he understands the pack area and you have begun the education of his mind, it is time to think about the requirements of his body as he is growing.

Chapter Summary

Your puppy needs a safe and secure bed, and a cage is an ideal choice: easy to clean, it can be moved easily, and in the car or on holiday your dog will always have its own home.

Your puppy will already have been taught certain rules by its mother, and it will expect these same rules to apply when it enters its new pack area, your home. It is a mistake to think that you are being considerate to your puppy by waiting several days to explain your house rules. A puppy does not need a 'settling in' period without rules: it needs it with rules and explanations. What it does in your home in the first week will be the way it expects to be able to behave in the coming weeks; you may try and change the rules, but how are you going to explain this change to the puppy who has 'settled in' with the old ones?

CHAPTER 4

A BALANCED DIET

Understanding the nutritional requirements of your puppy is as important as training him; an incorrect diet can give rise to problems that can seriously affect both your puppy's health and his behaviour. When a puppy is growing he uses energy, therefore he needs a diet that will help to replace the energy he is using. When his growth rate slows down he uses less energy, and at this point the energy in his food needs reducing. In order to maintain a balance you must adjust the 'energy in' (food) to match the 'energy out' (growth): if the food is out of balance and the 'energy in' is not reduced to match the slowing down of growth, the puppy will have a surplus of energy. This surplus energy can be utilized by the puppy's body, causing it to grow too quickly and possibly causing joint problems, or it can cause a puppy to become overactive.

Because all breeds and sizes of puppies and adult dogs have different requirements, it is not possible to provide information on any specific diet. Even if it were possible, *telling* you what to feed your dog would not be as helpful as *explaining* why and how to feed for different growing and exercise needs. For example if I were to explain the energy requirements of a small breed of dog, these would be entirely different to the requirements of a large breed. The former will soon reach its adult height, but the latter may still need growing energy for the first year or eighteen months of its life, depending on its breed.

You can soon see why it is important to research the breed of your puppy before you bring him home. Even if you have a rescue or are not sure of the breed, the bone formation and size of the puppy will help you determine in your own mind what his adult size will be. After all, you will not be buying a puppy with absolutely no idea whatsoever of its mature size!

To begin with we have to look at the different food that is available: minced meat for dogs, tripe, tinned meat, dog biscuits, complete foods – these are just a few to be thinking about! We all have our own preferences, and what works for one person and their dog may not work for another, so let us look at the options. Usually by a process of elimination coupled with common sense it is often not too difficult to select the best diet for your dog. Most brands of food make a range of puppy food, followed by junior food; after that comes adult food with all its variations, and some brands will also provide a senior food for older dogs. If you study the labels on the packaging, and complete foods are usually easier to learn to 'read', you will notice that the main difference is in the energy levels in the food. The easiest way to 'read' the energy level is to look at the protein and fat, or oil, content. When these levels change, so may other ingredients, but they will all form to create a

Puppies need a good diet to keep up their energy levels whilst their natural energy helps them to grow. If they receive a higher level of energy in their diet than is required they can become hyperactive.

balanced and nutritional diet – but for a specific purpose. So a puppy food will have a much higher protein and fat level than a junior food, and this in turn will be higher than an adult food. We would, of course, expect the vitamins and so on to be different in food manufactured for a growing dog, but these will be balanced with the other ingredients.

Now what we need to think about is the purpose of the higher energy percentages in the puppy and junior food. The higher energy food is geared to provide the puppy with the energy it needs to grow, or rather to 'top up' the energy it is using to form strong bones and tissue. So if we now look at this factually you are feeding your puppy a food not to make it grow, but to keep it healthy while it grows. There is a huge difference, for if you feed to make it grow you are not feeding naturally: your puppy will not be growing at a natural pace to a natural size, instead it will grow too fast and in some cases will be a larger mature dog than nature intended. If you

feed to keep your puppy healthy while it grows, you are actually helping your puppy to grow at a steady pace but to remain healthy at the same time.

Recognizing your Puppy's Nutritional Needs

If you think this sounds complicated and fear that you will never understand it, I can assure you feeding is not difficult if you keep a common sense attitude, and it is well worth whatever extra effort it takes to get it right. You may be surprised when I tell you that almost all the consultations I do for owners with problem dogs will reveal the dog has been on an unsuitable diet, and that none of those are of too low an energy diet!

First of all study your puppy: how fast is he growing? The average medium-sized dog will almost treble in height in the first three months of its life; after that it will slow down, and between approximately three and six months it may double in height. These are approximate growing periods and sizes. If you now think of these growing periods as stages in your puppy's life when his natural energy levels are working overtime to supply him with growing energy, then it becomes clear that during each of these stages your pup will benefit from a nutritional boost in his diet. Now it is not so difficult to work out how to alter your dog's energy level to suit his requirements. From weaning to approximately three months the average puppy of medium breed will grow quickly, so it will need an energy boost in its food; its growth will then slow down, so its energy intake needs reducing. At six months it will have done most of its growing so its energy intake must be reduced accordingly. By one year old it will also have begun to fill out and its energy requirements are now for exercise and not growth, so its food must now cater for maintenance. A smaller breed of dog will reach its maximum height far sooner than a medium breed, and a larger breed of dog will have longer growing periods. It is now easy to understand if I say that a small breed of puppy may have reached its full height when a large breed at the same age is still only a puppy build.

It is important to try and understand nutrition, as incorrect diet can lead to joint damage when a dog literally outgrows its own frame. High energy diets that are not utilized correctly can irritate internal organs and can also make a dog appear to be hyperactive. Let us look at this with a common sense attitude again. If you feed your puppy a high energy diet to keep him healthy while he grows, but you don't lower the energy level of the food when his growth slows down, what is he going to do with all the excess energy you are feeding him? You don't have to be an expert on canine behaviour to work out that he will have a greatly increased energy level. So take, for example, a medium-sized dog: at three months its growth period slows down, but you don't lower its energy intake; at six months its growth rate slows down again, but your puppy is still on the

Puppies will play games with each other using their teeth, but they should never be allowed to tug at sleeves and trousers as a puppy that is over-active may take some controlling.

same food it was eating when it was eight weeks old – and it is now beginning to feel a little intoxicated with all this energy. You may lower the energy intake at six months, or you may continue to feed the same explosive diet for another few weeks: either way the damage is done. Your dog is coming up to adolescence – and we all know this is the time he will test the boundaries – and he has so much energy he doesn't know what to do with it: and there you are, trying to tell him to behave himself! How easy is it to get teenagers to listen to reason when they are intoxicated? It isn't easy when they are sober!

You now have a guideline for why and when to control the energy intake, and as we have used a medium size to explain you can see how it should be reduced sooner with a smaller breed, and increased and for longer with a larger breed. These are guidelines, and some dogs may take longer to develop than others, and some may need more, and some less, additional energy. If your dog is full of energy to the point of being bad mannered or is hyperactive, look at his diet, because you are probably feeding rocket fuel!

How do You Know What to Feed?

Breaking down the growing stages and explaining feeding and nutrition in this manner makes it easier to understand and also helps to dispel some of the confusion and myths surrounding canine diets. If you go into a pet food shop you will be surrounded by gaily coloured bags and tins of dog food all proudly proclaiming to be the best. Their prices will be as varied as their packaging – and remember that each brand will tell you it is the best: well,

each individual brand may be the best for some dogs, but it may not be for yours. So let's break it down to help you decide what is best for you and your dog. To begin with, don't assume that the most expensive foods are the best. There is only so much that dog food can contain. Just like human food, you may think you have a bargain at a little under the odds, and be cautious at a little over the odds, but you don't pay well over the odds for something that has an average value. Pet food manufacturers are catering for all breeds, so if their food advises feeding a puppy until it is six months old it cannot reasonably mean every breed of puppy. You may not have understood that a short while ago, but now you can begin to understand how to look at the information and then adapt it to you and your dog. Feeding is common sense, so whatever information you receive, make sure it is applicable to you and your dog's requirements before you apply it.

There are many dried or 'complete' dog foods on the market; these are mixed and balanced for you, so all you need to do is feed them. But don't buy a product because it is 'new and improved' or 'now with special whatever-is-new-on-the-market'. Don't be confused by the varieties. And don't buy food because it looks good: *you* are not eating it! You may prefer to buy tinned food, but what appears to be low protein on a tin may actually be quite high when you take away the moisture content. Many books and trainers will advise you to feed naturally and I would be one of the first to agree with this, but it really isn't as easy as it is proclaimed. For a dog to eat naturally, as it would in the wild, it would not be eating anything containing any form of preservative, it would not eat anything that was polluted, had been fed

Puppy 'Ben' is playing with a lead he has found; he is outside and enjoying himself, but he has seen something that troubles him.

antibiotics, been killed by a human, or been fed on a manufactured diet. So if you are feeding meat or tripe that is as pure as you can imagine, I bet the cow it came from was not fed on a holistic diet. Plenty of fruit and veg. is natural, but in the wild the fruit and veg. is not carrots and apples, it's roots and berries. So whichever diet you choose to put your dog on, think carefully and sensibly, don't follow fashion, and don't feed a particular brand or type of food because someone who 'claims to know' has told you that you simply *must* feed it. Check it out first, find out whether it is a good food for your dog, and whether or not the dog belonging to the person who recommended the food is a well behaved and healthy dog. I have had people contact me with a problem dog, and have discovered that its diet, which is exacerbating the problems, was recommended by a friend; but when we delve a little further it will emerge that the friend's dog also has a behavioural problem.

Feed your puppy to suit its energy and

His brother 'Pip' wants the same lead and a game of tug ensues. This is a harmless game between puppies and they are learning hunting skills, but when played with a human being there is the danger of a puppy believing it is being encouraged to use its teeth.

growing requirements. Most puppy foods range between 27 and 33 per cent protein, and if you feed a higher one, then consider aiming to reduce the level sooner rather than later, as you will have been putting more energy into your pup, thus encouraging faster growth. Learn to 'read' the labels, and try to provide what a dog would eat naturally – but keep a sensible, common sense attitude. For example, dog owners will often tell me they feed their dog on a diet based on chicken and rice, or lamb and rice. This sounds healthy, as it is the type of diet humans may consider to be healthy, but in the wild, dogs will not be roaming on a rice plantation. So although they are feeding healthily, they are aware that they cannot feed as naturally as in the wild, so are having to consider the next option. Vegetarian diets are available for dogs, and vegetable energy is lower than meat energy; and although dogs do eat meat, they also enjoy vegetation – and if a dog has a naturally high energy level, it is worth considering all the alternatives to reduce the energy supplied by food. At the end of the day, you are the one dealing with your dog – you will be the one that has to try to calm it down when it is bounding full of energy after eating food that makes it feel intoxicated. You will be the one that has to try and teach it manners, and any well meaning people who advised you to feed your dog the way they thought was best will not be around to help. So think carefully about your puppy's growth rate, listen to advice, read books and learn as much as you can, but always listen to what your puppy is telling you. If his growth speed has slowed down, his body is telling you to consider changing the energy intake. If he has so much energy he finds it hard to sit still and to listen to you, then consider how much is natural energy and how much may be induced by incorrect diet.

A puppy rarely needs an increase in nutritional energy, as the first year is a steady decrease as the growing slows down; however, when a dog has reached maturity, the energy food can be reintroduced if the dog is going to be using more energy. Nevertheless, few pet dogs will use so much extra energy that they need to be given a boost. The time to really change the food of the adult dog is with the seasons, and few people remember this. In summer a dog may spend a lot of time out of doors with its owners, but in winter it will spend far more time in the house or the garden. Thus in the autumn, begin to

Any games involving teeth should be delayed until the dog is mature enough to be sensible. This picture shows a mature dog with good manners playing tug with an adult, but imagine what could happen if an unruly dog tried to 'tug' a lead from a child's hand. Be very careful how you play with a puppy and monitor his energy to avoid him becoming over-excitable when he is playing.

lower the energy intake so that by the time winter arrives your dog is already calm and prepared for some cosy nights in. At the time of year when people are busy rushing around preparing for seasonal festivities their dogs are often behaving like delinquents. My telephone in the early part of each year is red hot with frustrated owners wondering why their dog is practically climbing the walls with pent-up energy. Feeding is not just as simple as putting food in a dish and serving it up; I know of many dogs that both can, and will, eat anything and their lucky owners never have a moment's trauma with them. However, I also know of many frustrated and worried owners whose dogs have become a real problem, and although the reasons for the dog's behaviour will be varied, there is always one common denominator: incorrect diet.

When and Where to Feed

There are no set rules other than somewhere peaceful and private to eat, and with adequate time between meals for the puppy to be able to digest and utilize the food correctly. I'm sure you would not like your dinner plate on the floor with large and threatening feet wondering around, any more than you would benefit from meal two being given to you shortly after meal one because it happens to suit the waiter to serve it this way. Provide a safe place where your puppy can eat in peace without distractions or disturbances.

You should also allow him time to eat it, but do not leave it down for him to keep returning to if he does not eat it all at once. Just as you are going to provide him with regular meals, he must learn to appreciate them and eat them when they are provided. You will do neither of you a service by allowing him to dictate how he will conduct his mealtimes. If he can return to eat when he wants, you will not know when he is ready for another meal, nor will you be sure how much he is getting, as his meals will merge into each other. If you allow him to dawdle over his food, he will learn how to be fickle and to manipulate you, for you will find yourself wondering if the reason for his slowness is due to boredom with the food – and of course if you change it, he will gulp it down because it is different. Before long the process will be repeated, and you will find your clever little puppy making you change his food regularly and threatening to go on hunger strike if you don't jump to it!

It is a big mistake to keep changing brands of food for the sake of it, or because you think your puppy is bored with the present one. Dogs do not become bored with food, unless of course they are told they can choose what to eat. Dogs in the wild will eat meals similar to human meals before the advent of convenience food, namely meat and two veg. I was brought up on good old-fashioned dinners, and only in recent years have I found them to be dull, purely because I am now converted to take-outs, bags, packages, and any other way I can find tasty food that takes no preparing. I'm spoilt, and I like to tantalize my taste buds, but I also put weight on when I do; so do your dog and yourself a huge favour, and find a good nutritional food for him and stick to it. If he occasionally decides he doesn't feel like eating it, then maybe he is not particularly hungry, maybe he has a stomach pang, maybe he simply doesn't want to eat anything at all for while. One thing is for certain, he is not sitting there thinking 'I

Your puppy may have been used to eating with his brothers and sisters, but when you take him home make sure he can have some privacy when he is eating. Provide him with an area free from other dogs, cats or people walking past him.

don't want to eat this food any more, and I will refuse to eat ever again if you don't supply me with a new menu'; but if you keep changing his menu, he will very soon expect it. Within a range of one product you may change energy levels several times, as your puppy grows and from season to season or according to exercise when he matures; but each brand of food provides different energy levels, so to change the energy you do not change the brand or type, you simply choose a different level of the food you are already using .

When your puppy is on multiple feeds a day – four, down to three, and then two – you will space them out during the day; but when he is older and getting just one feed a day, supply this at a time that is best for both of you. It is always best to aim to make sure the evening meal is not too late, as you will be hoping to keep him clean and dry during the night. Similarly when he is on one meal a day, don't provide it too late in the evening. You feed your dog when you want to because you are the pack leader; it is your home and you are the provider, and it does not matter a jot whether he is fed after your meal or before it. The only way this makes a difference is if the dog associates your meal time with his, when he may begin to drool or even demand; if he sits and waits patiently until you have eaten, it is because he is well mannered, and not because you are eating first. Yes, in the pack the pack

It is not unnatural for dogs to eat vegetation, but be very careful what your puppy has access to, because not all herbage is safe, and puppies like to experiment with different tastes; this puppy has managed to get to a plant despite the efforts of his owner to provide him with a safe area. Never leave a puppy unattended for too long as he will get into mischief.

leader eats first – but are you running round a field catching a rabbit and devouring it with your dog? If you are, then he must be made to wait. And if you are teaching your dog to sit at the table and use a knife and fork, then yes, he must wait until you have eaten your meal. I think you will be getting an idea now of how to keep a good dose of common sense handy when you are bringing up your puppy. When you use the pack instincts, they must be how a dog perceives the pack law, and not how human beings translate it.

I have read and heard about many different opinions on feeding, titbits, and different methods of making sure you can take away a dish of food from your dog without it showing any sign of aggression. But why would anyone want to keep removing a dog's dish of food? This one has always had me baffled. In theory it is to ensure that the dog is not possessive with its food or dish, and should someone touch, move or pick up the dish, the dog will not be aggressive. The method is to remove the dog's food before it has finished, and then return it to allow the meal to commence; in some instances the food is removed more than once during the same meal. However, I know that if someone kept removing my meal it would make me very aggressive; in fact I would be extremely annoyed, and would neither like nor trust the person doing it. Furthermore in practice I know of far too many aggressive dogs that have been made worse by the deployment of this method by their owners. On the occasions

There is a lot to be learnt from watching natural animal behaviour. Ben and Pip are playing in their own little grass area: they have found something they think needs closer investigation and Ben is the adventurous one. But when Ben was called away, Pip continued with the detective work on his own. He is learning to be an individual and not to be dependent on brother Ben.

this practice has had an effect, other than exacerbating the problem, it has served to make the dog submissive and, rather than looking forward to its meal, being wary of any offerings. As with any form of training some ideas work and some don't, but if you want to ensure you have a good chance of something working, look to the pack for answers. A pack leader will not keep removing the prey from one of its subjects; it will allow it to eat but if for any reason it does want to remove it, it will do so. It is the pack leader, the decision-maker, so it is entitled to do so. The theory of making sure your dog does not resent anyone else removing the dish of food looks a little weak if you remember that your dog is the lowest ranking member of your pack, so it will respect all other members of your family. You are also bringing this puppy up to have manners and to show respect, but I fear that if you tease it with its food you may lose its respect rather quickly. It needs to be able to trust you and to know that you are the provider you are supposed to be, so give it the respect of a valued pack member and have faith and confidence in your ability to teach it good manners and to show it good parenting.

Titbits

This is one of my pet subjects and I have often received criticism for my strong opinions on the proffering of titbits to teach a dog how to behave. I can only reiterate that in my opinion bribing a dog to do something is not teaching or educating it. I never bribed my children to be well mannered: I educated them and then expected good manners from them, not only if they had a chocolate bar first. I am not adverse to titbits, indeed, I often wander around town with dog biscuits in my pocket that I forgot to empty, but if I give them to my dogs it is because I feel like offering a treat occasionally, not because I cannot get them to do anything for me without one. Neither do they expect a treat; if they get one, it's great but if they don't life's still great. Instead of using food use your voice and your body actions, and when your puppy pleases you tell him you are pleased with him. Giving a child a sweet for doing something may be a nice treat but where's the pride in pleasing mum or dad? A smile and an acknowledgement of how clever the child is and how proud the parents are will mean more and command more respect and effort next time from a well mannered, respectful child. So it does go full circle: if you want a respectful puppy treat it with respect. If you treat it with respect it will become a respectful puppy.

One final word on food before I close this chapter. If you have children, do not allow them to share their food with your puppy, do not allow your puppy to lick or eat from plates or to lick fingers, and make sure that your children understand the importance of not giving any titbits. A puppy is a young, impressionable canine and if children play with it and feed it titbits there is a danger of your puppy seeing them as young canines. If in his eyes they become littermates to him he will interact with them as a littermate, and as such he is entitled to nip them. This advice applies to dogs and children of any age, but in the case of a puppy what may seem like harmless fun when it uses its teeth will be dangerous in just a few short months when it has matured. If it has played roughly, pinched food from plates or snatched food from children's fingers it will perceive you as having allowed it to do this, so when you want to change the rules when it is bigger it will not understand. Rules must be clear from the onset and you can't change them because your puppy is now bigger than it was when you first made them, so make sure you think in front. Prevention is better that cure.

There is no such thing as waiting until your puppy is a certain age before you teach it how it should behave. Training and good manners should not be confused: training is extra curriculum, but good manners should be taught from the beginning. The education of a puppy is not to be taken lightly and the learning curve is extended to you as well as your charge, for as he develops you will learn how to communicate with him and how to guide his instincts to your advantage. It's time to learn about how to teach good manners in a language your puppy will understand.

Chapter Summary

The energy level in a puppy's diet must be balanced to match the energy it is using to grow. If the energy 'in' is higher than the energy 'out' a puppy can develop problems. Joint problems and overactive behaviour are often a result of incorrect diet. There are many different types of food to choose from, but learn to read the labels and choose carefully, remembering that dog food is manufactured for dogs in general but each breed grows and develops at a difference pace.

Provide a peaceful place for him eat and allow him to enjoy his meal undisturbed.

Do not use titbits to teach him how to behave: he must learn to respect you and not what you are going to give him.

CHAPTER 5

FOLLOW MY LEADER

Young dogs are just as impressionable as young children, and learn by watching and copying. A puppy will watch its mother and copy her, the way she eats, chews a bone, digs; in fact everything she does, the puppy will try and emulate her. If she is not around it will copy its littermates, but as they, too, are learning about life and behaviour there will be no strong messages for the puppy to pick up. It will learn to interact with the rest of the litter as they all pick their way through all the instincts they have, trying and testing them until they find what role in the scheme of things they can play in their puppy games. If there are senior canines to learn from, a puppy will delight in watching and copying; but although the litter games are fun, it will strive to be accepted by the grown-ups.

A lot can be learned by studying the natural behaviour of puppies and their elders. In the previous paragraph it is not difficult to see what role a human must play to gain a puppy's respect, and how failure in this role will lead the puppy to seek elsewhere for guidance. If your puppy sees your interaction with him as that of a littermate, he will perceive you as being no more mature or better informed than he himself is. He will enjoy experimenting with his instincts and even his teeth as he uses you to prove his role in the puppy pack – and the role he is likely to take will be that of puppy leader. If I tell you that

even if *you* were puppy leader you would not have a worthy senior pack status, you will understand that if your puppy sees you as a mere puppy pack member, then he will consider you as having absolutely no authority over him whatsoever. You may feel you have control, but as he matures he will gain in confidence, and with every ounce of confidence he gains, the more areas of your life he will try and take control of. Add to this any surplus energy he may have from his diet, and he will steamroller his way into adolescence with you as a mere hanger-on, hoping for some recognition along the way. If, when you are reading this, you have a sweet cuddly puppy fast asleep beside you and you think he could never take over your life and your home, I can assure you that he will. If you are very firm in your assurances that he *can* make his own decisions, that he *can* treat you as an equal and run your home for you, then he will grow up to be obedient and do just that: the fact that now, what he is doing is not what you want is irrelevant – if you have always led him to believe he is the leader, then believe me, he will be.

Whether small or large breed, a puppy that thinks it is in charge is quite often an accident waiting to happen. It may be chewed carpets, it may be a ruined kitchen, it could be aggressive, or it may simply be that your dog does not come back the first time when you call it. The latter may seem like a minor misdemeanour compared to the others, but if your dog is running towards a road and you cannot stop it, then a road accident and a dead dog can be the result. Does this sound harsh and dramatic? Well, we all think it's never going to happen to us, but it doesn't matter what breed it is, if a dog does not respect you enough to come back when you call it, then it *can* happen. The education of a puppy cannot wait until it has made its own rules and you want to change them: what he does as a puppy he will expect to do as an adult. Therefore as his pack leader and senior canine mentor, you need to give him some sensible guidance and pack rules.

Subliminal Training

Teaching a dog to understand what you are saying is not easy. So often the normal state of affairs is that eventually, and after much repetition, you will see a glimmer of recognition in your puppy's eyes when you say certain words. However, while you are struggling to make your puppy understand you, valuable time is being lost, and if one word is repeated ten times in order to get your puppy to sit, then the next time you ask him he is quite in order to wait until you have again repeated yourself ten times. It is not unusual for owners to tell me their dog is finally getting the hang of lead walking: 'It only pulls a little and it won't be long before we've mastered it.' But the problem is not the fact that the dog hasn't quite got the hang of it, it's the fact that the dog is nearly two years old. This is not unusual; but remember my four non-negotiable commands – walk behind, stop, wait, and recall? These are not only the four most important ones, but the *only* four you need in order to have a well mannered dog – but they are often the last to be taught. Yet the dogs that struggle to see why they should do these simple tasks for their owners will often excel at retrieve and ball games.

If you can stop your dog, make him wait where he is, bring him back to you at the first call, and keep him sensible on a lead, you can take him anywhere and know you can control him. If, however, if you have to repeat these commands when you are on your own with him and there are no distractions, then you have little chance of him listening to you when there may be something more interesting for him to take notice of. The secret is to not repeat the commands in the first place: if you want your dog to do as you ask on the first time of asking, then you must make sure you only ask once.

So how do you do it? Think about how you would explain the word 'sit' to someone who did not speak your language. If you kept on just saying the word it would be meaningless, so you would encourage them to sit, either by demonstrating or sitting yourself, and would invite them to do the same. When their attention was focused on the action and when they were actually performing the action, you would say the word 'sit', and that person would now relate the word 'sit' to sitting down. If you had said 'sit, sit, sit,' they would think the action was called 'sit' multiplied by three, because they only know what you tell them. In the same way, if you made a mistake and said the word 'rainstorm' when you should have said 'sit', they would think that 'rainstorm' was the correct word. Even if you explained you had made a mistake, and had given them the wrong word, for a long time the word 'rainstorm' would come to mind when they sat down.

Now think about your puppy and what you are teaching him if you repeat or change your mind about certain words. He is only learning certain sounds that you give him, and if you get it wrong you do not have a human language that will enable you to explain your mistakes. Try not to think of your commands as words, but rather, as sounds. For example, if you always call your puppy to you in a low tone, and then suddenly change it to a shrill tone, it will seem to him like a different sound. You may have used the same word, but it will be difficult for him to grasp this – he is learning, and he is not able to read your mind: he does not have a 'dog/human' dictionary to fall back on, and he does not need to try and understand you. He has his own way of going on, and if you want to change this to your way, then you must make the communication easy for him to understand.

Subliminal training means getting your dog to do the action, and then providing the sound you want him to associate with that action. If you train by using the word first and then trying to get the dog to do the action, you will find that action and command do not come together: the timing of the command so that it follows the action is vital for the dog to associate the one to the other. Now let us use this method to teach your puppy the four non-negotiables.

First of all decide what words you are going to use. 'Sit' and 'down' are two separate actions; you may want to use 'wait' to tell your puppy to wait outside or inside the house, or in the car; and to keep 'stay' as a command for him not to move until given permission to do so. Your puppy must learn to walk behind you and he will

If you push your puppy down to make him sit he will probably resist and push upwards against you. If you say 'sit' whilst he is resisting he will associate the word sit with pushing up.

need a command for this action, but a different command should be used to bring him to your side in the 'heel' position. If you are thinking of training your puppy for any of the disciplines when he is older I would strongly recommend that in his early training you do not use any of the commands you are likely to need for this. I have already mentioned that good manners and training are not the same: good manners are stopping, staying, recalling, and giving the respect of walking behind you. Training is 'extra curriculum': retrieving, hand-shaking, ball games, and the education needed for any of the disciplines – it is extra; it is optional and not mandatory. Good manners are mandatory: without them a dog will lack respect and concentration, and will eventually become a problem.

Teaching a Puppy to Sit

'Sit' is an easy command to teach, but resist the temptation to push your puppy

With your hand under your puppy's chin or on his chest, gently push him back and he will begin to lose his balance.

down into 'sit' position. If you push his rear end down he will resist and push up, and even if he does not resist he will have sat because you pushed him. If you put your hand under his chin and gently push him back he will *think* 'I need to sit'; and as he sits, you say the word. Don't make an issue of repeating this over and over again, but spend a few moments gently showing him what you want, and then give him a chance to think about it. A few moments regularly are far more effective than intensive education; puppies will learn very quickly if you keep their lessons short, simple, and easy to understand. It will not take long for your puppy to associate the sound to the action, so that when you say the word 'sit' he will think 'I need to sit'. If he does not sit straightaway, do not repeat the sound: simply move as if you are about to ease him back into the sit position, and he will anticipate what you are about to do and will sit; then tell him he is a good lad. This is a wonderful, simple way of teaching, and the end result is a puppy who sits at the first time of asking.

Teaching the Stay

You will be spending a lot of time with your puppy during the first few weeks of your life together. You need to get to know each other, and of course puppie's grow very quickly, so every moment you can spend in his company, enjoying his formative months, is wonderful. But use this time wisely: interacting and playing is fun, but it must also be educational. In the wild no

Here Pip is beginning to think he needs to sit down, and when he is thinking about sitting he is asked to 'sit'.

Now Pip will soon learn the 'sit' command, because each time he sits he will hear the instruction; however, he has not yet completed his little task as his mind is on other things.

moment or action is wasted, and you will do well to follow this canine rule. Each time your puppy waits for a second or stays in a position long enough for you to use it as part of education, you should then provide a corresponding sound. Your puppy will often stop and look at something or wait a second before entering a room or when investigating something, new, so give him the 'wait' command. He will already be familiar with 'wait' as you use it prior to giving him permission to leave his cage and enter your space. When he is used to 'sitting', place your hand gently on his head and ask him to stay; get him used to this gently, and once again do not overdo it. Never try and cram too much information into your puppy too soon; if you are sensible, over a period of time you will be able to move a short distance away and your puppy will stay where he is. This is not a competition, there is no race to be won – all you are doing at the moment is laying a foundation of good manners that can be built upon at a later date if you wish to introduce a training programme.

As far as I am concerned, to train a puppy too soon is robbing it of its youth. When I rear a puppy I expect it to show me

respect, so it must observe the four non-negotiables: it stops, stays, walks behind and recalls when asked to do so; but its puppy and adolescent years can then be spent growing up and maturing at a natural pace. I rarely train a dog before the age of one year old, but I have never had a puppy or young dog that I could not take anywhere and be confident it would not show me up. Good parenting allows a child to develop at the pace they can best learn at, not at a pace that is dictated by others; similarly your puppy needs to feel confident in you, and if it sees you as its pack leader, it will. Pack leaders make the decisions, but they know that a youngster who is too dominant or too nervous is of no use to the pack. All education is aimed at producing the balance needed to ensure a good pack member who is also an asset to the pack and not a liability.

Teaching the Recall

The importance of the recall command is often grossly underestimated in a puppy – but if you cannot get it to come back to you when it is young, what chance have you

Now that Pip is giving his undivided attention, he can receive praise. Notice the gentle hand on Pip's back making sure he does not interpret praise as an invitation to get up.

got when it is a cheeky adolescent? Let me tell you a story as a dog may see life.

> *Once a week I take my humans to the park – I have to drag them there as they are usually very slow. When we get there I leave them and go and chat to other dogs and enjoy myself, but I always have to go back to them because they are frightened to be left on their own. I know this because they keep shouting for me. When I get back I put them on a lead so they feel safe, but I often have to drag behind to slow them down because they can't wait to get back home.*

This story always raises a chuckle, if only because many people can identify with it. If a dog is allowed to feel it is in control, then it will take control. Don't wait until your dog ignores you and runs off chasing rabbits, people or other dogs to realize it doesn't have a recall: teach it one when it is a puppy, and make sure it understands it. When I ask people if their dog has an instant recall I am usually told it has, *if* 'it does not see another dog, . . . is not too far away, . . . it cannot smell rabbits' – in which case it doesn't have an instant recall, does it? If you call your dog twice it will expect you to call it twice, if you usually call twice you will soon find you are calling three times and it will expect you to call three times. You are not explaining to your dog that when you call it, you expect it come to you at the first time of asking, and that this is not negotiable. If you negotiate over every command by repeating it several times, your dog will expect always to enter negotiations before doing anything for you. It is far more difficult to teach an older dog an instant recall than it is a puppy, so begin as you mean to go on.

Choose a word for your recall, and don't use your puppy's name as part of it. His name is to address him and to get his attention, it is not a command. 'Come here' and 'here to me' are two examples, and I

Ben understands the 'sit' instruction and responds as soon as he is asked; he has also learned that he does not stand up until he is given permission. Here he is wanting to see what Pip is doing, but is being asked to 'stay' for a minute; he will then be given permission to go and play. He is never asked to concentrate for too long – that way he never loses concentration.

am a big believer in using more than one syllable. 'Come here' is two and 'here to me' is three when they are rolled together as one word. If you use your dog's name you would be saying 'Fido come', but the name would be used for every command, as 'Fido sit', 'Fido down', 'Fido come'. This is undermining the dog's name, and is also wasting two syllables. I object to using just one syllable, such as 'come', because it is not very definitive, has no tone or rhythm, and can soon be lost on a strong wind.

You will find during the first few days that your puppy will always want to be with you, it will never be far away and there will be times when it sees you and runs towards you. Subliminal training means that you always tell your dog what it is doing, so each time it runs towards you, give the sound you want it to associate with wanting to be with you. My recall is 'that will do' but rolled together it forms one word, 'thatlldo' – so each time a puppy thinks 'I want to be with mum' and runs towards me, it hears me say 'thatlldo', but I only say it once. Eventually I can say the word 'thatlldo' and it thinks 'I want to be with mum', and runs to me. If it doesn't come, I go to it and gently bring it to me.

This is an important part of making sure your puppy has good manners and that it respects you. His mother will already have taught him that when she called him to her, he had to come. Why should you command any less respect? He will expect you to give him clear guidelines, it is part of his canine instinct. But now let us look at another instinct and one that plays an important role in ensuring your puppy sees you as his pack leader. The space immediately in front of you is your space, and your puppy will not expect to run into that space uninvited. If you were following

a tour guide in a museum and he stopped and turned to talk to you about a particular item you would not keep walking until you were directly in front of him: you would respect his personal space and stop a few feet from him. Your puppy at some point will respect your personal space and stop a few feet from you; if you then lower your body and coax him to you, he will see you as a pack member rather than a pack leader. When he pays you the respect of waiting to be invited, do not lower your position, but turn your back and bring him to your rear, then turn around and make a fuss of him. Once again, use the pack instincts to help you train: a pack of dogs will not fall into line in front of their leader, they will come around the back of him. Similarly a tribe of Indians will not return to the chief and stand in front of him, they will fall in behind him. Your dog will understand that if he is expected to

The recall should always bring a dog behind, and not in front of you. You are the pack leader and a dog will not enter that space uninvited. A recall is not an invitation, it is a recalling of a pack member into the safety net of the pack. Meg is learning two commands here: 'stay' tells her to remain where she is, and 'come here' brings her into her handler's space.

fall in behind you, then you must be hierarchy to him: it is pack law. Calling your dog to come and sit in front of you is fine after he understands that a recall brings him back behind you. It is easy to teach and just as easy to stop him a little in front of you and call him to your front as part of extra training at a later date.

It is easy to misunderstand the pack instinct, so always think carefully before you act. For example, if you turn and walk in the opposite direction, your puppy will panic a little at losing contact with you and will make sure he keeps an eye on you in future. But this will not work with an older dog, as it will see it as a game. If your puppy does not come back when you call him, and you are certain you have explained to him that he must come back first time, and he understands this, then go to him and gently bring him back to where you called him from. He is impressionable, eager to learn and just as eager to please, so take advantage of this willingness and in the first few days you will be well on the way to him understanding the four non-negotiables.

Teaching your Puppy to Walk Behind

Just one more natural rule to learn and I have left it until the last, as your puppy will be aware of it but *you* may not as yet understand it fully. Where does the pack walk in relation to the pack leader? Where is the Indian tribe in relation to the chief, the pride of lions to their leader, the army to the general? They all travel behind their leader: they do not walk one head length in front, they do not even walk at the side, they are behind. This is what is expected of the pack, and it is what a pack member

This little chap is on his own now, his brothers and sisters have all gone, but he is quite happy trotting on behind his owner's feet. He is safe and protected, and knows that when he is given permission to go in front it will only be when it is safe for him to do so.

expects to be told to do. Your puppy will have been told to walk behind his mother until given permission to go in front, and it is up to you to make sure he continues to give you this same respect. He will not come into your house and bound everywhere in front of you in the first few moments, he will stay with you, and will go behind you if he is unsure of anything: he is on new territory, and he will automatically look to you for reassurance and for leadership.

Provide this security he needs by giving him what he expects to see, and don't pick him up and push him in front to other people, don't encourage him to go ahead and investigate on his own; this comes later. Go ahead and invite him to follow you, go through a door and invite him through after you, go and investigate whatever he is curious or nervous about, and invite him to check it out when you have made sure it is safe for him to do so. Small and simple actions, but they are so important, they will send clear messages to your puppy that you are the leader, the decision-maker, the protector. Far from making your puppy nervous because he is not doing his own investigating, it will make him feel secure in the knowledge that he can rely on you for leadership and clear rules. The time for him to investigate on his own is when he has a pack area to identify with and a leader he can trust. As with a child, you will encourage him to find things out for himself, but only when you know this is safe for him to do so; the child then understands that whilst he is learning and satisfying his curiosity, it is with your sanction.

As with all actions, you need a sound to tell your puppy what he is doing, when he is keeping 'behind' you. Once again you can select any word or words you wish, as for example 'back', 'keep back' – if you were to say 'fishnchips' your puppy would associate it with keeping behind you, although *you* may not; in short, it only understands what you tell it. I would strongly advise not using the word 'heel' for this action, for several reasons. To begin with, when selecting a sound to use for a command choose something you can identify with, and something that is easy for other members of your family to relate to. Secondly, you will eventually need an instruction that will bring your dog forward into the recognized 'heel' position; and third, you may wish to join a dog club when your puppy is a little older, and 'heel' is usually the recognized command for walking at the side.

When your puppy passes you, gently lift him back behind you and say 'behind'; never attempt to keep him there for any length of time: he is learning, and does not need pressure. Make sure you give him permission to go in front of you when you are ready, rather than allowing him make

his own decisions. He has not yet earned the right to live in the grey area, and he is not mature enough to be able to make sensible decisions. When you feel you have made your point as to who is the senior canine, give your pup permission to enjoy free time. Think of parenting and teaching: a child must learn the right and the wrong way, what is acceptable and what is not. The sooner this black and white area is established, the sooner the grey area can be used.

At no time should you be putting pressure on your puppy; he is young, he is impressionable, and he expects to be part of a pack with a pack leader. Use this information to teach him: his youth makes him dependent, being impressionable means he will copy and learn, expecting to be part of a pack means he will recognize and respect a leader if the messages are clear and simple.

Now let us look at what we have achieved: first, a puppy who knows which is his personal space, his bed. He knows that to chew things in your space is not acceptable – he does not get told off, or shouted at, or experience any form of stress, he simply is not allowed to chew in your area. He does, however, know that chewing is permissible in his own area, and he also knows what is acceptable to chew. Sitting and staying, or whatever words you choose to use for him to stop and to wait, are becoming familiar to him, and as he never hears these words repeated, and he only hears them at certain times in conjunction with certain actions, their meaning is quite clear. He knows that each time he runs to you he hears a certain sound, and now when he hears that sound he wants to run to you. You are a senior canine because you are teaching him how to behave in the pack, and you are also the pack leader because you are the one making the decisions and you are the one he walks behind and respects.

In all this you have laid the foundation for a well mannered and biddable puppy, and all without having to raise your voice; it has taken only a few days, and you need not teach him any more commands for a long time. All you need to do now is to make sure you do not become tempted to lower your pack position by repeating these commands as he becomes a little older and tests your pack boundaries. These commands are non-negotiable, so make sure he doesn't make you negotiate.

Mental and Physical Boundaries

Teaching boundaries is easy; teaching a dog boundaries when it has already made its own is difficult. You have already started to explain some of the boundaries to your puppy by telling him which is his area and which is yours, and you need to decide where you are happy for your puppy to go, and what areas you want to be out of bounds to him; you must also decide which boundaries may seem safe but can cause problems later. To begin with, do you want your puppy to have access to upstairs, or to your bedroom area if you are in a bungalow? It will not spoil your puppy if he goes upstairs: being allowed to go to a higher level will not give him hierarchy status, but if he is going to go upstairs, he must not be allowed to go up ahead of you. The house belongs to you, and you can show him your pack area and you can invite him into any part of your area, but it remains yours. If he does not respect it, he must return to his own area to think about it. If you have children I would recommend you make the puppy's boundary at the bottom of the stairs; you cannot be around all the time, and children can often incite a young dog into misbehaving.

If there is an area you do not want your puppy to have access to, you must make sure he does not gain access to it. A puppy will not see the best room as being out of bounds because he is carried into it rather than allowed to walk in when you want to show him to friends. Rather, the friends must go into a room that is within *his* bounds; you can explain the situation to them, but you owe it to your puppy to keep his rules simple and clear.

When he goes into the garden make sure he is behind you when you go through the door. Making him sit and wait does not establish who the leader is, it simply means he sits and waits, and the fact that you are going through a door does not come into the equation. Eventually he will pick up the fact that when there is a door he has to sit and wait, but as part of an exercise, not good manners. Do you tell children to sit down while you go through a door? No, you tell them to follow you through it and not to push in front. You are already teaching him the 'behind' command, so all you have to do is make sure you go through first; he will be happy to follow to begin with, so use this time to give him the appropriate sound.

In the garden he will be able to enjoy the freedom to go anywhere, but if you don't insist there are boundaries you may be making a rod for your own back. You will, of course, need a good perimeter fence; when puppies gain confidence they become more and more inquisitive, no hole will be left unexplored, and the space beneath a gate will be an invitation to escape. However, if your puppy has the

Puppies must learn where their boundaries are, and if a fenced area can be provided for them to play in they will not only be safe, but will not regard the area outside the fence as theirs. Glen and Moss watch as people walk past the garden fence which is a few feet from their boundary; this helps them to feel secure, and discourages them from barking at passers-by.

run of the garden with no rules he will assume the garden is his area, and as such that he is entitled to dig where he wants, and when he is older to choose whom he has in it. Dogs fence running, jumping up at gates, barking at passers-by, or nipping people in the garden are all dogs that have been allowed to 'own' the garden – which means that they are not really committing any crimes, since they are the decision-makers in the garden. Provide an area within the garden that your puppy can have as his own personal 'do what I want to' space, and then allow him to use the rest of the garden with your permission. No one should be allowed to invade the puppy's own area, and particularly not children or strangers: it is the equivalent of his cage or bed area in the house. If you provide an area inside and an area outside for your puppy to play in without being told 'no you can't do that' and 'no you mustn't do this' he will be happier and more contented than a puppy who is never

sure what he can and can't do, and where he is and is not allowed freedom.

Puppies are great mimickers – in fact, dogs of all ages love to copy – but puppies learn by copying; thus if you lie down they will lie with you, if you jump up quickly so will they, if you move with jerky movements so will your puppy, and if you are relaxed and laid back in your approach to training you will have a happy and relaxed puppy. He will not be an angel, but then neither are you, and he is emulating you! If your body language is stiff and erect he will see it as anger, if you are bending and yielding you will appear submissive. A pack leader is strong, but within that strength there is a suppleness, grace and gentleness that is approachable. You must appear to your puppy as being capable of protecting him and of being able to make all the right decisions, but you must also be there for him whenever he needs you. Never ignore him: even if his behaviour is attention seeking, do not ignore him. You can ignore his behaviour, you can ignore his attitude, but do not ignore *him*: how can he trust you if you reject him? Pack leaders never ignore their subjects unless they are treating them with such contempt they no longer want them in their pack! A parent may ignore a cheeky song, but they will not ignore the child singing it. Remember you have a mirror image, and if you are going to ignore it, then expect it to ignore you!

Stressful Situations

Stressful situations are unavoidable, but even if the situation is stressful, your puppy does not have to be stressed. For instance, it is the first visit to the vet and you are apprehensive; there are other dogs in the waiting room, so you hug your puppy to you, telling him it's all right. You are about to see a needle inject him and you are stressed, your body is tense and your voice is different – and your puppy is mirroring you. When you get home you will probably think your puppy was nervous of the vet, and he probably was, but only because you told him to be and, what is even worse, you also told him *you* were nervous of the vet! To begin with, why are you apprehensive? It's your decision and it's no big deal, he trusts you and he is not going to get hurt. Hugging him to you will convince him there *is* something to be nervous of, whereas what he needs is to hear your normal tone of voice talking to him. As for the needle, it's not injecting you, so why are you nervous? It's up to you to keep your puppy relaxed so he will not be tense, and then he won't feel a thing.

You are walking down the road and another dog is approaching you, so you pick your puppy up to protect him. What are you protecting him from? The other dog will probably not have taken any notice of him, and if it did, holding the puppy in front of you is not protecting him: it may feel to you that you are offering protection, but you are actually transmitting to your puppy that you are nervous of other dogs. If you feel it wiser to stay away from the other dog, do so calmly, and if the other dog is passing you, put yourself between it and your puppy. If at any time you need to pick your puppy up to offer him protection, don't tell him why you are doing it. For example, a dog known for being aggressive is approaching you and you cannot avoid close contact, so calmly pick your puppy up and walk on as if nothing unusual or worrying is happening, and talk to him in a normal voice. If at any time your puppy does have a fright, when everything parental and protective is screaming to you to pick him up and seize this opportunity to cuddle and coddle him, resist it and give your puppy the strength and calmness he needs. Pick him up by all means, give him a love by all means, but keep your voice matter-of-fact and allow him quickly to resume whatever it was he was doing. If not, you are in danger of him always being frightened of whatever it was that caused the upset.

Showing the Way

Where do you want your puppy to sit? It may sound like a simple question but what does not seem to be a problem in a puppy can be a major problem when it is fully grown. A small puppy cuddled up on a cushion on your settee may appear cute, but I bet you won't think that when he is fully grown, covered in mud and grinning

Everyone loves to cuddle a puppy, but cuddles on furniture as a puppy can lead to an adult dog sitting on furniture. If you are not going to allow him on furniture when he is older, do not let him go on it as a puppy. A puppy can enjoy lots of cuddles sitting on someone's knee on the floor.

all over his face as he dries off by rolling on your best furniture. Even if you have him on your knee on the furniture when he is a puppy, you cannot justifiably tell him off if he gets up there on his own. If you don't want him on the furniture, don't let him get on it right from the start, and don't encourage him to think he can sit on your knee on the furniture. You can give your puppy lots of cuddles whilst sat on the floor with him, and this cannot lead to any misunderstandings by him. Size will determine many of your rules, if you have a very small breed you will probably be content with him sitting on the settee and he will probably not be covering it with mud at a later date. The larger the breed, the more you must consider what you are, and are not, going to be able to allow when it is mature. If you have an old suite and are intending to replace it you cannot allow him on the old one knowing you are

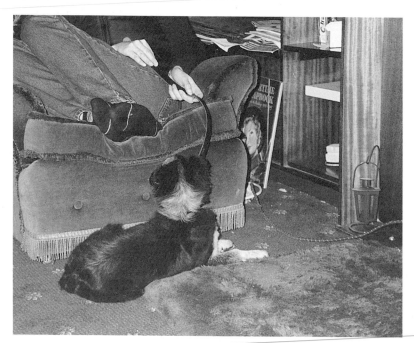

Ben has never been allowed on the furniture and here is on a lead while he learns to sit and be patient. It is important for puppies to learn to have a 'quiet time'.

Ben has settled down and fallen asleep. A puppy will play as long as someone is prepared to play with him, but too much excitement will result in over-tiredness; like a young child, a 'winding down' time is needed. Ben will soon learn to settle down in the room and enjoy a peaceful time.

going to refuse him access to the new one; he won't know one was old and one is an expensive new one, they're all the same to him.

I can remember someone complaining to me when their puppy was ten months old that it had ruined their kitchen, and because she had bought the puppy from me and I had supplied feeding and training information, I was mortified. I asked her why she had not contacted me earlier as I provided a follow-up service, and since puppies don't suddenly turn into monsters overnight, there must have been some warning signs. She informed me she had been happy to let it chew the old kitchen as she knew it was being replaced! The reason it had chewed in the first place? She had ignored my training advice, thrown my dietary information away, fed a high protein diet and had given it a box full of toys to play with – and this lady had come to me with references!

Incidents like this helped to dissuade me from any breeding programme other than my own replacements of young dogs as my oldies retired.

There are breeders who do not provide a follow-up service and breeders who do not breed for compatibility, but my heart goes out to those who breed conscientiously, providing good youngstock, and then suffer the backlash of those who have disregarded their advice. No one knows their line better than the breeder, and every little foible and characteristic can be explained. But I also feel that many owners of puppies are left in the lurch after purchasing for a considerable sum something they have spent a long time looking for; they are given insufficient information from the breeder, and are left to the mercy of manufacturers of wonder gadgets and the shops selling them.

Everything you do with your puppy is to show him, in a gentle but firm way, that you are the leader; once this is established your puppy will always be attentive to you. Whatever you do he will be watching, though don't encourage him to watch you to the point of not thinking for himself. He needs to be attentive to you, but he also needs to be an individual. Training is for later, it is extra curriculum and usually for something special such as a discipline. Good manners are essential and begin the moment your puppy enters your home. Living with your puppy and discovering each other's characters, learning to understand one another and communicating, is ongoing and is fun, and can go hand in glove with teaching good manners.

Chapter Summary

Puppies love to copy and they will look for a senior pack member to emulate; they also expect to see a strong leader.

There are four commands needed to teach good manners; they are non-negotiable, and once learned you do not need to teach any other commands until you are ready for 'extra curriculum'.

Puppies should never be pressured, and once they understand their place in the pack and they have learned good manners, they should be allowed to enjoy their puppyhood.

A puppy is like a mirror image: if you have an aggressive body language it will reflect in your puppy, if you are calm and gentle you will have a calm puppy.

Provide mental and physical boundaries for your puppy. If you have areas in your home where he is not to go, make this clear from the beginning to avoid confusing him; similarly make it clear what areas he may have access to – furthermore, you must make him understand that *you* are allowing this access, and he must not take it for granted

CHAPTER 6

FUN AND GAMES

It isn't all hard work and orders. If you follow the pack rules there is nothing hard about teaching good manners – in fact your puppy will hardly notice you teaching him anything, for it will all be ongoing and a part of his everyday life. The only time it will be difficult for you is if you do not make a commitment to making sure he understands who is the leader. Sometimes it may seem easier to let things slide and to ignore occasional displays of bad manners, but it will be difficult trying to re-educate him when he is a wilful adolescent.

I enjoy having fun with my dogs and my puppies and I also love playing games with them, but you may wonder how I manage it when I do not have frisbees, toys, tuggy games, titbits and other numerous gadgets designed to keep dogs amused and occupied. It is simply that I am their fun and their amusement: I do not train with special collars, gadgets, clickers, titbits and toys, and I do not have bunches of keys and pebbles in a bottle to distract them because I am the one they should be concentrating on, I am the one they should be interested in and I am the one they should be listening to. While a puppy is learning to understand my rules, to identify me as the pack leader, and has bonded with me as its guardian and best friend, it does not need a box full of toys to distract it. It will have a bone, and a warm and safe bed, and I will spend as much time as I can with it during the first few days – but it won't all be spent interacting: I will also sit and watch it, and talk to it, and study its movements and its body language. It will watch and learn and begin to develop its instincts, and I will study how best to develop these instincts to my advantage.

A ball is an unknown quantity to a puppy, and left to its own devices it will invent its own games. Ben is not sure what it is, but he discovers that when he touches it with his nose it moves!

Unable to resist the lure of a possible game, Pip comes forward to investigate and between them they discover the fun of rolling a ball. Two puppies having fun, just as one puppy and one human being can interact with a ball – but allow the puppy to discover a game rather than tell him what to do.

To find out more about my puppy I will introduce a small ball into a game, but will not have a preconceived idea of what it should do with it. A ball to a puppy is not an article to be retrieved, or to run after. We often tell a dog what to do, and don't allow it to use its own initiative. When a puppy first sees a ball it may be apprehensive, but will certainly be curious and will want to investigate. I've seen puppies touch a ball with their noses and then jump back and watch it when it moves; a second investigation is usually a little bolder, and eventually they are pushing it around with noses and paws. This is where the initial training of 'no chewing in my pack area' can help you teach your puppy some really good games without any danger of encouraging him to chew or to be destructive.

One puppy of mine, Mossie, was introduced to a small ball, and at first sight she

Mossie has developed her 'patience skills': she will wait and try and tempt me to move one of the balls first.

When the game finally gets under way Mossie flicks one ball under her stomach and picks the other one up. Her patience pays off.

regarded it almost as if it were a scentless mouse. She stalked it and finally pounced on it, running back when it rolled away from her; then her next encounter saw her bravely pushing the ball with her nose, and then just sitting and looking at it. Up to this point I had been an amused observer, but I decided to join in and give her something to think about. I lay opposite her on the floor with my arms outstretched and pushed the ball towards her; she mimicked my position by lying down, and when the ball rolled between her front legs she rolled it back with her nose. I took the ball back and rolled it to her again. This time she picked it up in her mouth, but made no attempt to chew it: she just held it. I then produced a second ball of the same size and rolled this to her. She dropped the first ball and picked up the second one, whilst I immediately took possession of the first ball. I rolled the first ball back and took possession of the second ball when she dropped it in favour of the first. A few repetitions of this action and Mossie began to think, she watched me carefully, and as I rolled my ball towards

her she dropped the one in her mouth, flicked it underneath her and picked up the one I had just surrendered to her. Clever dog, she had worked out what was going on and had thought out a plan of action that outwitted me – and all this had been done in silence. Dogs think best when they are quiet, but when she figured out how to beat me the game was relaxed and she received a 'good dog' for being clever without being dominant.

We often play this game now, and she is three years old. She doesn't retrieve or play any rough games, and I have never encouraged her to do so because she is very excitable and would soon become hyperactive if she were allowed to play without thinking. The only difference in the game now is that when she is waiting for me to make my move she will make a crowing sound if I don't get on with it fast enough. I have also watched her when I am not in the game with her, and she will study her front paw for some time, opening and closing the pads, and then she will put an open paw on the ball and flick it away, almost as a human would. I often see her studying my hands when I am making her wait for the ball, and I realize that now she is trying to copy what I do. This is a lovely way to play with a young pup, and this kind of game can still be played when the dog is an adult, in a field, on the beach, at home, and hardly a human word needs to be spoken.

Do Dogs need Toys?

No, not really. They do need to be able to amuse themselves, and if they are in the garden they will soon find something to do and something to play with. It may not be what their owner had in mind, so to provide them with a source of amusement rather than let them find their own may be a good idea. But supplying something is where it should end, for a dog will never learn to amuse itself and invent games of its own if it is constantly being told how to play. If you provide a large quantity of toys your dog will not learn to concentrate, it will interact between the toys and will never settle to playing quietly and constructively. It really is not a matter of what we, as humans, want or how we think it should be: we are dealing with a canine, and in the pack all canine games are educational. A mindless or repetitive game is not constructive, but a game that makes a dog think and use its skills is a game of education with a calming influence. Think of a child who receives a present and then spends hours happily playing with the box it came in; furthermore the child will be using its initiative with the box, as there is no obvious game to play.

It is not my intention to be a spoilsport by giving a list of things you must not do and by recommending you must not use toys. There is nothing wrong with the concept of using toys; it is better for a puppy to play with something clean and safe that is under your control than something it finds on the ground that could be dangerous. But I do advocate quite strongly that you think very carefully about *what* you use, that you use whatever you choose sparingly, and that you do not oversupply. A lot of money can be spent on 'dog accessories' and it can cost a lot of money in behavioural fees trying to correct the damage caused by too much, too soon, and too often. Squeaky toys are a popular choice, but in my opinion they often serve to take the part of a mouse, rabbit or other prey a dog may have fun in tormenting. They also can cause a dog to be so wound up when making the noise, that it becomes hysterical and destructive – and on a personal note, constant squeaking would drive me mad. However, when a puppy of mine had to have a cast on her leg at only seven weeks old, I gave her a squeaky rubber carrot which she had hours of fun with when I was busy and she was on her own. Because of the cast on her leg she was on zero exercise and couldn't play with the other dogs, but the first time she squeaked it in front of her canine family her grandmother calmly removed the squeak!

Beware the Danger of Toys

You may decide that, even having read my opinion on toys and how I recommend stimulating a puppy's brain rather than just its body, you still cannot resist buying toys. But I would like to point out that however much fun a toy might seem, it could be a potential danger.

Any toy can be a danger if a dog chews and eats it. A teddy bear may appear harmless, but a teddy bear's ear lodged in a puppy's stomach can be life-threatening.

Soft cuddly toys may seem harmless, but why would a puppy need a soft toy? Is it for it to cuddle up to? If this is the idea the teddy may serve as a surrogate mum during the night, but the puppy is probably far more likely to chew or suck it. I know of two cases of older dogs who had teddy bears as puppies: one suffered intestinal problems and had a life-saving operation, and the other died, and both had chewed and swallowed teddy bear ears as puppies; the ears had lodged and had eventually caused horrendous problems. I know of three cases of a dog having to have an operation for gut problems, and in each case pieces of a rubber toy had to be removed from the gut. I know of one case of a puppy swallowing a 'dog toy' that

actually swelled inside the stomach and the puppy died. I know of several cases of puppies having toys and balls lodged in their mouths and throats. I know of many cases of dogs with hip and other joint problems due to too much chasing, twisting and turning after balls when they were young and their bodies not fully developed. Frisbees are only a variation on a ball, they are thrown and the dog jumps up in the air to get it. Balls are thrown and a dog runs, skids to a stop and swerves to bring the ball back. I know of several cases the same as the previous ones, but caused by the puppy being allowed to play with an older or larger dog that played roughly, thus causing damage. I have lost count of the cases of aggressive dogs that I know that have had their problems caused or exacerbated by being allowed to play tuggy games in their formative years, and have learned to enjoy using their teeth.

If I know of only one case of heartbreak there will be others, when I know of several cases there will be many others. I know there will be far more puppies that have not had a problem with any of the above than puppies that have, but if only one in a hundred has a problem it is one too many. So please, if you are going to provide toys for your puppy, think very carefully about what you choose and do not allow it to chew them.

Alternatives

So what alternatives are there, and what other games can you play? You do not have to be committed to playing games all of the time; simply being with your puppy, talking to him and stroking him, is valuable interaction. Learn to enjoy his company and encourage him to enjoy being with you, not for the games and the food you offer him, but because you are you. Set a value on your own company, and he will value you. If you turn yourself into a mobile toy box and vending machine you cannot expect him to respect you. You don't need to be holding a toy up to make him sit, you don't need a ball in your pocket to ensure he comes when called. Do you want him to come back to a ball or to you? I sometimes think if someone from another planet watched dogs being exercised in the park they would be certain that the dog's owners were round balls and the transport was on two legs!

Learning to Lead-Walk

Your puppy needs to learn about a lead. Another 'problem' area is when a young dog is so bad on a lead that the owners let him run loose rather than train him. They don't see a problem as they have a field at the back of the house, and if they go to the park they take him in the car, so they don't see any point in teaching him to lead-walk. But lead-walking is not just to enable you to get a dog from one place to another, it is a means of ensuring that he walks from one place to another in your pack and with

Introduce your puppy to a collar and lead as soon as you can. Pip understands 'sit', 'stay' and 'behind'; and he is now being shown how to walk behind on a lead. A gentle hand under his chin lets him know he must not move forwards yet.

respect. It is also to make sure that at no time can he be a danger to himself or to anyone else. The dog that has not been taught to walk correctly in the pack will not have a recall either: as far as he is concerned he doesn't need one because if there is no pack to walk behind, then there is no leader to call him back. But, what happens if there is an angry dog or person, or there is a deer, sheep or horse rider in the park? No recall and no lead equals no control!

So get your puppy used to a collar as soon as possible; he may scratch at it at first, but if you take his mind off it, he will soon forget it is there. Take him out into the garden and show him an area where he can dig: this will enthral him, and the collar will be unnoticed. When he is used to the collar, put a light lead on him and let him get used to the feel of it on his body. You can leave it trailing behind him for a few minutes for him to get used to the slight pressure on his collar. He is used to

Pip stands and waits and has no problem with keeping behind until his pack leader considers it safe for him to run free. The body language of the handler must always be flexible and friendly.

following you, so pick up the lead, keeping it light and gentle. When he sits and sulks and tugs backwards, ignore him, but don't let him go back and don't try to pull him forwards. He will eventually get bored of sitting and come towards you, and if he doesn't, make a sound he cannot resist, almost as if you are whining; he will then move towards you and you can praise him, though be careful to keep your back to him – if you face him you are teaching him to be in front. One of the first things to learn about dogs is that confrontations provide

Meg is used to walking behind, and she is used to the lead. Her body language is pushing forwards and she has a cheeky lift to her tail. The lead held upwards, but not pulling, reminds her she is not to push in front without permission. All puppies test the boundaries, and it is up to us to make sure we keep giving them a gentle reminder.

losers, and you cannot afford to lose, so you always avoid having a confrontation.

Patience is all that is required. If you start pulling and tugging you are providing ammunition for your puppy to argue with you. Never ignore your puppy, but ignore his tantrums; be aware that he is there and talk calmly to him, and he will settle – and when he does, tell him he is a 'good lad' and go a step forwards. If he reacts again, just stand and wait patiently. You will be a lot more patient than him, for his curiosity will not let him sulk or his tantrum last for long. This is the most awkward scenario, but most puppies will settle to a lead within a few minutes, especially if you have been encouraging him to walk behind and have been giving him a command for it. He will recognize familiar actions and words when you put the lead on, and this will give him something to understand.

Interacting with your Puppy without Toys

Out in the garden you can find many ways to interact with a puppy without using any toys. As mentioned earlier, you can provide him with a 'digging area', as dogs love to dig – and because they love to copy, if *you* begin to dig you will soon find you have a willing helper. You can provide a sandpit or a section of the garden, give him a 'no' when he digs in the wrong area, and a 'good lad' when he gets it right. Bury a bone and dig it up with him – it may sound a strange thing to do, but people expect dogs to play human games, so why shouldn't humans play canine games? You are not going to continually keep digging up his bones, and of course his instinct will tell him how to bury them; however, if he

Pip is used to playing with a ball on his own and will use his teeth, but he will not chew it.

had an older dog to emulate he would watch and join in 'digging school'. Some dogs love water, and if your puppy is one of these, half fill a washing-up size bowl with water and let him splash his feet in it; you can join in with your hands. Make sure you don't do anything he doesn't like, don't let him play in deep water, and don't overdo it to the point of him becoming excited and not actually playing. There is a big difference between play that induces learning, leading to a contentment, and play that induces excitement leading to hyperactivity.

There are many games that can be played inside; the one that I play with Mossie is excellent for quiet mind education. Three plant pots and a ball can be used to play 'find the ball', and the same game can be played by hiding the ball

Rob does not use his teeth unless told he can pick the ball up.

Here you can see how Rob uses his nose to push the ball, just as puppy Ben was doing; it is easy to give a puppy a command to 'roll' rather than 'pick up' because this is the first thing it will do. If taught to play gently and creatively as a puppy, the result is an adult dog that is safe to play in any company without becoming over-excited or using its teeth.

elsewhere; you can also use this method for teaching which part of the garden is for doggie play and which part is the 'quiet area'. Keep these games quiet; as much as a child will find it difficult to work out where something is hidden if it is running round in a state of excitement, so will a dog. Don't be misled into believing a dog has to be barking and running around wildly to be happy and having fun. All dogs will have a 'silly time', and it is good for them to let off steam; and it is also good for them to realize that as much fun may be had if they do it on their own, or without senior interaction. A pack leader will not join in the 'silly time', he will observe and make sure it does not lead to an accident or to arguments if there is more than one dog involved. In this way your puppy will learn to use his senses to tell him what is going on around him. He can see, hear and smell, but his senses will not relay the same messages to him that your senses will relay to you.

Learning to Use his Senses

Sight

Whatever you see, your puppy will see it quite differently, and there will be many things that you take for granted that he will be able to see. Try getting down to his level and seeing the world as he sees it: thus feet at close quarters can be quite a threat, and they all smell differently; furthermore feet that keep moving are ideal for chasing, and even better for nipping – so those feet are teaching your puppy how to bite! Your kitchen will look entirely different from the floor, and a high step in a doorway will block from view what lies beyond. In the garden, *you* see the tops of flowers and the lawn, whereas he sees flower stems and the creepy crawlies that wander around under the grass, and the tiny hole in the fence that you didn't notice will be like the Grand Canyon to him! Even when he is fully grown he will never see the world in the same way that you do: your vision is different, therefore so is your view and your expectations of what is to come. Keep this in mind, and never take for granted that your puppy or dog knows what you are wanting of him; he could be looking in the same direction as you, but could have an entirely different train of thought.

Hearing

Some dogs have keener hearing than others depending on their breed and ear shape – but whatever the breed, providing there is no impediment, your puppy will have better hearing that you. When you see someone walking towards you your puppy may not, but he will have heard them – he will have picked up the sound and the vibration of the footsteps probably before you are aware they are there. You may have seen them but because you are also seeing other things and your mind is just as busy as your sight you do not take any notice, seeing someone is not the same as noticing them. So imagine someone is walking towards you but is still a distance away, your sight has passed across this person, seeing but not really accounting for him. Your puppy hears him and reacts either with fear, apprehension, joy, or just unsure what to do. By the time the person has actually been noticed by you, your puppy is already in a state of excitement or fear.

Learn to take notice of all that is around, so you can be aware of anything that may affect your puppy if it comes near to you or it makes a noise. For instance, if you are in the country you may see a tractor in a field; in a built-up area he will have the constant sound of traffic, but in the countryside the noises will be different and he may not be expecting a loud and unusual engine noise. You have seen the tractor, so rather than wait until your puppy is surprised and shocked, prepare him without alarming him. You are the pack leader so he trusts you, so ask him to come into pack position behind you, and if the tractor is behind you, turn around: always place yourself between your dog and anything that may surprise him. Don't talk to him in a voice any different to your usual tone; if it is possible to keep walking, then carry on as normal; if not, stand and wait until all is clear, then carry on as if nothing has happened.

Only pick him up if it the safest thing to do, as picking him up can often alert him to something unusual, and you are then placing him between you and whatever may surprise him. And if you turn so that he is away from the problem, then you have also turned your back to it. Thinking of it logically, you are offering him the security of your pack, so you must always be facing the front; and if you leave your puppy outside your 'safety net', a sudden surprise noise will upset him. This shock can also make him unsure of how safe you are to be with, whereas when you bring him into the space behind you it will convey a message of 'there is something in front my leader needs to deal with'. This done correctly with a puppy that sees you as leader, will result in a puppy not being frightened of tractors. The same goes for wagons, cars, motorbikes, anything that on first meeting may cause a sudden shock.

Don't wait until someone knocks at the door and he scurries off in fear, or becomes so noisy you cannot get him to listen to you. If he is unsure or fearful, simulate a door knocking session to get him used to the noise of knocking; then when someone is actually at the door, let him have a quick bark, which is his way of saying, 'Someone's at the door', then ask him to be quiet while you let them in. Once in, he must wait until he is invited to say hello. Few visitors can resist a puppy jumping all over them, and they will want to pick him up and cuddle him – but I bet they won't be amused when he is big and they are dressed in their Sunday best! It only takes a minute to make him sit and wait before being invited for hugs and cuddles, and that minute can save embarrassment later and will prevent your pup from growing up thinking he has the right to frisk all your visitors.

Smell

This is the important one, and the one you really need to understand. Let us go back over the previous scenario in which we saw someone walking towards us but did not actually notice them. When we put all our senses together we will still not have noticed this person – but the puppy will have heard him, and his other senses will already be working. He can also smell this person, and what he smells will be dependent on what the approaching person is thinking and not on any artificial perfume. A person changes smell with each mood, so a scent will change several times a day and can change in a few short strides with a change of mood. When the person sees the puppy (and the puppy probably still cannot see them) they will react. If they

don't like dogs they will not give off an offensive smell for the simple reason that a puppy is considered harmless so they will ignore it; therefore the smell will not be threatening. Most people will smile and feel friendly towards a puppy, so the smell or scent is warm and reassuring. Your puppy hears and is unsure, sniffs and feels more confident, and by the time the person is in his sight, you and the approaching person are relaxed so the message to the puppy is one of safety and he will probably receive some attention from the stranger. This now makes it appear to you as if your puppy is socializing, but in fact he has made his own decisions based on information received through his senses, and you just happened to go along with the decision.

Things would be different if the approaching person had been carrying an offensive smell; it could be working clothes masking the real scent, there could be another dog involved, or it could be the smell of another dog on the person's clothing. The human beings may have the same attitude as in the previous paragraph, but your puppy is unsure, and the unfriendly approaching smell will cause him concern. As the other person draws near, you are concerned about your puppy's unsociable behaviour and the other person tries to stroke your puppy and reassure him that they mean no harm. In order to try and and make your puppy socialize you pick him up and hold him still while they stroke him. It seems so simple to a human, but to the puppy it is a different story: he is wary of the newcomer, the sound is coming nearer and the smell is strange, the sight brings an unknown person looming over them, and your attitude is worried and quite stressful. Now he doesn't like strangers and you are not a safe pack leader because you have subjected him to unwelcome advances.

You are on a losing track in both of these scenarios, the latter because it makes your puppy wary, and the former because it leads him to believe he can accept strangers, although he may greet the next stranger and be stopped short by scent and move straight into scenario two. Either way you run the risk of a nervous puppy, or one that mugs everyone it sees: the first one doesn't trust you, and the second one is not making use of its sense of smell and is literally jumping in before thinking – and one day this dog could hurt someone, or be hurt. In both cases you have failed to be a pack leader.

How should it have been handled? You see the stranger approaching and you call your puppy into pack position behind you. Puppy wonders why you are tightening your pack, and listens and smells. He hears the person and waits, he smells the person, and tells you by means of body language what he feels. If puppy and person want to say hello, they do so with your permission; and if puppy doesn't want to say hello, you respect his wishes. It doesn't matter if failing to allow a meeting will cost you your job, your best friend, or the chance of a prized autograph – your duty is to your family, your pack, your puppy. His body language will be easy to read, particularly as you will have been observing his moods and natural language every day: thus if he is scared he will drop his tail between his legs, if he has a short tail you will see his back end lower; if he is angry he will go stiff and his coat will stand up; if he is wanting to greet the stranger his body will relax, he will wriggle, and his eyes will carry a warm greeting.

Reading Your Dog's Body Language

Eyes

Never underestimate the power of the eye: your puppy will tell you a lot about himself just by looking. If he is nervous, his eyes will make quick movements and he will seek a place to run and hide. If he is curious his eyes will be bright and will look directly at whatever is fascinating him. If he is bold he will stare at you, though you must be careful not return the stare: there is a train of thought that to outstare a dog will prove you to be more dominant, but if you have to resort to staring to gain leadership by submission then I feel it to be sad, for both human and dog will miss out on so much. Look at your puppy by all means, but never resort to staring: a cold, hard stare to another human being would instigate ill feeling, and to do it to a dog or a puppy will not command respect. If your puppy does not want to look at someone, it is more than likely that he doesn't want to meet that person either, so respect his wish. If he stares at someone and appears almost to be hypnotized, he will probably be trying to use his gaze to create a fence at the edge of his 'fight and flight' distance. Respect his feelings and move him away.

'Fight or Flight' Distance

This is the space that we all have, that we like to keep between us and anything or any person that we feel threatened by. The same distance or space can also be used as a mark of respect; I call it the 'wait and see' distance. Imagine a perimeter around your puppy: anything outside that perimeter is in the flight distance, meaning that the puppy can turn and run if it is concerned.

Once the edge of the perimeter is crossed by something it is concerned about, it is in the puppy's fight distance. This means that it is too close to the puppy for it to turn and run, so it must stand and fight. Of course circumstances will alter the situation, but they will not alter the puppy's feelings. For example another dog may be outside the imaginary perimeter and in the flight distance, but when the puppy is on a lead it cannot take flight. If another dog enters the fight space your puppy cannot fight if he is on a lead. He is only a puppy but his instinct to survive will not desert him, and he will of course look to you for help and you can sort out the situation. But the situation should not have arisen, for as his guardian you should have seen what could happen and should have prevented it. Your puppy's body language, his eyes and the position of his tail will all have told their story. If you failed to see the possibility of this happening, you should be acting as soon as he begins to speak to you with his actions and bring him behind you into your protection.

The 'wait and see' distance is the same distance but for different reasons. This is the distance the puppy will wait in front of you when it is facing you rather than invade your space: it will wait and see if you are going to invite it forward. When it is approaching something it is not sure if you will approve of, it will wait and see what your reaction is before it goes out of your space and into the space of whatever it is curious about. Let us go back to following our tour guide round a museum: when he or she stops and turns round to discuss a curio, you and everyone with you will stop; you will all respect the speaker's space, for at that moment in time he is the pack leader.

This space is a silent distance; nobody draws it or discusses it, you just naturally

These dogs are creating their own game; they are using their senses to tell them what is around them, and their instincts to play as a pack.

Once the game starts, they use their distances to denote how they should play. The two dogs nearest the ball are on the perimeter of the 'fight or flight' distance of the 'prey' the ball, each one using its senses to try and outwit the other. The dog on the far side is at the 'wait and see' distance, but the two dogs nearest the camera have entered each other's 'fight or flight' distance and are challenging each other rather than the ball.

stop at the edge of it. Every dog has its space, and some need more than others – and their body and expression will change when this space is in danger of being entered. As a puppy, 'wait and see' will be far more prevalent than 'fight or flight', although at some time in most dogs' lives this important space comes under threat. If you have not learned to listen to your dog's language and have not taught him that you are a reliable and trustworthy pack leader, it can result in tears. When a dog feels it has been let down by its leader it loses faith in him or her, and when it no longer trusts its leader it makes its own decisions. So a dog attacked by another dog, because the owner did not read the situation, can end up being aggressive to other dogs as it decides to become its own pack leader. What does not always seem important when your dog is still a puppy can actually be the key to a confident adult dog or one that can develop problems as it matures.

A gentle hand is far better than patting and ruffling the coat.

Using Your Own Body Language: Finger Tip Touch

Just as your puppy learns to use all his senses, make the most of using your own. Don't rely on brushes, combs and stroking or patting to tell you much about your puppy, learn to use your finger tips.

Make a habit of running your hands

Resisting the temptation to pick up and hug and cuddle, sometimes it is better to give a gentle massage. These puppies are enjoying this affection and are making no attempt to move away or clamber on knees; this provides a golden opportunity to get to know the feel of your puppy when it is relaxed.

gently around your puppy's body, but do not be intrusive: you are not probing and investigating, you are caressing. Gentle massage is far more acceptable than patting and stroking, and can be therapeutic for both puppy and person. You will become familiar with the feel of his coat and his skin; you will know what are little lumps and bumps he has had from birth, and what are new ones. Massaging him will help him to relax, it will get him used to being examined when he goes to the vet, and it will form a bond between you as you spend quality time together.

Dogs have favoured areas for massage, just as humans do; nearly all mine love having their cheeks and ears massaged, and their top lip is quite a favourite as well. I have one dog who will go completely dreamy when I massage his front legs and feet, and another that will lie upside down for a feet tickle. I have found these spots by massaging and watching the response, rather than making a point of sitting spending 'a few minutes massage time' – this will rarely work. Rather like absent-minded doodling, massaging to relax a dog comes with patience and the enjoyment of spending time together.

So much to learn and so much to think about, there is little time to go out and take him to meet the world. But don't worry, because for the first few weeks this need not be your main criterion – building up a trusting relationship is more important at first. Only then do you have to decide what you are going to do with the rest of your lives together, and how to get started.

Chapter Summary

Dogs do not have to have toys, but a toy used with imagination can teach a puppy how to think and work out situations.

Toys can be dangerous if they are chewed, so do not allow a puppy to destroy, chew or suck his toys.

Learning to walk on a lead is important. A lead is not a means of keeping a dog attached to you, it is a means of teaching a dog its boundaries.

Don't expect a puppy to play and do all the things you want, be prepared to join in with things he wants to do, and teach him to be content with his own company by providing him with time on his own.

Learn to read your dog's body language and to see the world through his eyes. Remember that his senses will tell him things about people and things that you never knew existed.

CHAPTER 7

WHAT, WHERE AND WHEN

All puppies have to discover what lies beyond the pack area, but not until they are well versed in pack behaviour. Your puppy should come back when you call him, take notice of you and what you are saying to him, and you should be able to trust him not to approach other people and strange dogs without your permission. However well behaved he is at home when there are no distractions, he will not be quite as discerning when you take him out. However, if you have taught him a good solid foundation of good manners, respect and loyalty, there will be few places you cannot take him. He will, of course, test the boundaries, and if he is a little angel all the time, then he is not behaving like a normal puppy. I once commented to my children how, although they were often given to testing my patience at home, they never showed me up in public. They informed me that had they ever been tempted, I had given them 'the look', and whenever I have mentioned this to other parents it seems we all share a similar 'look'. This look or mannerism is something I believe comes not necessarily with parenting as much as with tutoring. You may not always be able to give a puppy a 'look', but you can let it know by tone of voice and body stance that it is not to push the boundaries.

All puppies have to discover what lies beyond the pack area, but without a recall they can soon disappear and get into mischief.

Health

When you get your puppy you should receive certain medical information from the breeder. You need to know when he was last wormed, and when he is next due for worming; most puppies will have been wormed once and sometimes twice before they leave to go to their new homes. A regular worming programme is important, and your vet will be able to advise you what to use and when. Even a healthy dog will need to visit the vet for check-ups and vaccinations, and many people like their puppy to have a health check sooner rather than later. I am not in favour of rushing a puppy to the vet in the first few days; he doesn't know what he is going for, everything will smell strange, and you relinquish him into the arms of a stranger when he is not yet entirely confident in his new home. Some puppies will welcome the attention and some will be indignant or shy. Not wanting to meet the vet does not mean you have a problem puppy, it simply means he is not ready to be introduced; when he is confident in you he will think differently. Your puppy has to learn to trust you, and you must be able to trust your vet: someone who will take the time to let your puppy settle and will handle him gently is worth travelling further to and paying a little over the odds for. Never take your dog anywhere – to a vet, a dog club, or a kennels – simply because it happens to be the nearest or the most economical, your puppy depends on you to choose wisely.

If your puppy is fed on a good diet there should be no need for supplements, so don't be tempted to buy pills and potions unless they are needed and have been recommended by your vet. Many puppies will eat what to them is tasty and to us is disgusting; thus the eating of faeces is not unusual, but can become habit-forming. Some puppies will eat anything they can find, and when it tastes good (lots of goodness in it if the diet is good) they will look for seconds. Never leave any faeces on the ground for any length of time; try to pick it up as soon as your puppy has done it. It isn't always possible to follow him round the garden every minute with a poop scoop, but you will soon find his favourite spots for doing it, and this will make it easier to find and remove. Sometimes a vitamin B deficiency can cause compulsive faeces eating, but this is not likely to be the problem with a puppy, it is more likely to be a case of 'it is there, so I'll eat it', in which case early removal will prevent it becoming a problem. Try not to make too much of an issue about anything your puppy does that is natural to him but which you are unhappy about, for he will soon learn to use it as a game and will try to beat you to it.

Until your puppy has built a strong immune system he will need vaccinating to help him fight any diseases and infections. There is a standard vaccination supplied by your vet and he will tell you what the vaccination is, how it is administered and at what age. There is a homoeopathic alternative to the orthodox vaccinations, but you will need to go to a homoeopathic practising vet, and once again he will explain how they work and what it entails.

Most puppies are robust little bundles; they can eat, drink, run and play, and they rarely suffer anything other than a minor upset such as a thorn in a foot or hurt pride when they tumble over. However, you will remember my explaining that a puppy will grow naturally but will use extra energy from its 'energy bank' to do so, and when

Pip and Ben will soon be living apart and leading separate lives, but they are both well mannered, they both come when they are called, and each one will leave the other if called separately.

you feed you are not feeding to make him grow, you are feeding to top up the 'bank'. Similarly a puppy's 'energy bank' can be emptied rapidly if it is subjected to long mental or physical training sessions, to too much exercise, to playing to the point of hysteria, or to interacting with other dogs or with human beings who are not well versed in senior canine guidance. Having an older dog does not necessarily mean it is a good senior canine; it will depend on how it was brought up and educated, and whether or not it is willing to be a teacher, or prefers to be a bully. If a puppy suffers a sudden shock or a fright, if it has a new experience that is wonderfully exciting, its body will soon use up its natural energy in order to keep its system up and running. Once this natural energy has been used, its body will begin to tap into its reserve

energy in the 'bank'. The reason why you feed to keep the 'bank' topped up is because you cannot fill it up quickly if it becomes almost empty, and like any bank, if it is empty it is useless, and the system becomes weak. Never play with, work or train your puppy until his energy begins to wain, and never allow anyone or anything else to do so, be it child, adult or another dog. Puppies that continually have to call on their reserves to combat fatigue become more susceptible to infection and disease, as their immune system cannot work to capacity. This is comparable to a human being who is overtired or stressed: their immune system becomes low, making them more susceptible to infections and disease. Puppies are fun-loving, fun to be with and to play with, and they are greedy for information, thus making them excellent pupils; nevertheless they are very young and very vulnerable.

Socialization

Your puppy needs to be confident and to be able go where there are other dogs and people, but in my opinion there is far too much reverence given to the word 'socialization'. In fact puppy socialization has become fashionable, and educating your puppy to be well mannered in company seems to be outdated. I tend to study facts rather than trends and I always look at what happens in the pack. Puppies in a pack are brought up with mum, they graduate to the adolescent pack, and when they are mature and sensible they have earned the concessions that go with the rank of senior canine. If two packs meet they do not all get together and have a party; if they mix at all they are cautious, and they certainly do not allow their young to enter what could be a volatile situation. It may be easier to draw the same parallel with a tribe of Indians: the meeting of two tribes will see only the elders communicating, there will be no interaction of youth until such time as the elders know there is no danger and the youngsters are sensible and well mannered and therefore not likely to cause embarrassment or instigate bad feeling.

When I was a child I cannot ever remember being taken into crowded areas, groups and clubs, or being made to stand while people looked at me in order to become socialized. My parents taught me good manners and acceptable social behaviour, and when I was taken out I would meet people – but there were some people I did not particularly like. In fact I can remember being quite alarmed at one

It is very daunting for a small puppy to have someone towering over them. Try to imagine how you would feel if you were him: he is looking up into a face, the voice is being thrown down at him, and he is not sure whether to look at face, hands or feet.

person who had a loud voice and loomed over me like a giant, and I also remember running behind my mother and her holding her arm out at her side almost like a barrier. He was a very nice person, but I just didn't happen to appreciate this at the time; but the protection and parental reassurance I received soon eased my mind, and the next time I met him, although I was cautious, I began to feel more relaxed. A puppy is no different to a child when it comes to socializing and feeling protected.

If you rush your puppy off to join various groups and classes in order to make sure he is well 'socialized' you may find you are creating problems that will manifest themselves at a later date. Some puppies may be nervous of the company of other dogs and people, but most will dart off into the throng of puppies and become oblivious of you. You are encouraging your puppy to mix with other packs, since each puppy from a different home is from a different pack, and if he is not yet a respectable member of your pack and does not know you are the pack leader, then you have lost him. If you were in a room where some people were of a different nationality to you and you could not understand their language, and others were your own nationality and you could understand all they said, who would you interact with? You would automatically lean towards the people you could understand with the least effort, so why should your puppy take any notice of you when there are several there of his own kind, all speaking his language and all having fun?

You may have a plus from this interaction, of a puppy who loves to play with other dogs and is not nervous of them, but you may have a problem when he is an adolescent and thinks all dogs are there for him to play with. I have seen dogs become nervous and aggressive because they have been the victims of a dog fight when they have tried to force a much larger dog to 'play' with them against its wishes. It could be argued that the aggressor should have been 'socialized' – but why should he put up with a young canine thug whom he doesn't know, invading his space. I know when I take my dogs on the moors for a walk and we meet another dog, I usually have to call mine behind me and make them sit down whilst a red-faced frustrated owner tries desperately to stop his dog pestering mine. My dogs neither want nor appreciate these unwelcome advances, but they do leave it to me to sort it out. I usually listen to the owner explaining to me that his dog only wants to play, when what he really means is he cannot get it to come back to him. Once again we can draw a parallel, for if I were to go for a walk and a total stranger ran up to me and began to molest me I would be furious and he would probably end up under arrest.

So what is wrong if all dogs are socialized in the same manner? It is not just the socialization of the puppy that causes problems, it is also the fact that whilst the puppy is interacting with other puppies it is usually putting them before you. He will enjoy his time with the other puppies, but if you cannot get him to leave them and come to you at the first time of asking, then he is giving them a higher status of importance that he is giving you. What we need to remember is that we are humans and dogs are dogs. People from different countries will have different cultures, but the one they have studied and that is part of their ancestral heritage is usually the one they will rely on for social information, and they will find it extremely difficult to fit into a new culture without a common language. A dog and a human have different backgrounds, cultures and social expectations, and no matter how well you get on with your dog, he will not eat with a knife and fork and he will not use and flush the loo. Neither will you gallop across a field after a rabbit with the intention of killing it with your teeth, you will not run around with a ball or a bone in your mouth, and if you ever tried to chase the postman you would probably be placed under lock and key.

Allow your puppy to develop within his own instincts before you try to teach him things outside of his natural expectations. If he is allowed to mix with other puppies when he is too young, and before you have instilled firm pack rules, this would be without senior canine guidance. He will be associating with other youngsters of his own kind this can make a puppy wayward, as it can a child growing up without parental guidance. A dog needs to identify with its own canine culture and it also needs to understand and control its natural instincts. You must encourage and control this before allowing him to integrate too often with other youngsters and before trying to teach him to understand and learn human behaviour.

You do not send children to pre-school without teaching them manners, and as much as possible about words, letters and games. Before they go to junior school they already have an understanding of how school works, and of how to conduct themselves. I can remember when my children were in their last year at junior school, the teachers gave them fifteen minutes homework each evening. Some of the parents complained about this, as it was not part of the junior curriculum. The teachers explained it was not compulsory, but it was to get the children used to doing a little extra schoolwork in an evening in preparation for the next school where homework *was* compulsory. Similarly, before we send our children to school we make sure they know they have a good solid family foundation with rules and boundaries to be kept to. We know they will be mixing with other children, and we know they may be tempted to copy them, so we try to make sure they have an understanding of right and wrong. They go to school to be educated, not to learn about family manners. A puppy should only mix with others when it is well mannered and respectful to its pack leader. If you are having difficulties in one particular form of training and feel you need help, I would recommend you seek professional help from a qualified trainer on a one-to-one basis. Whatever problem your puppy is developing, it will not be helped by allowing it to mix with other puppies where it may pick up more bad habits.

If you want to join a club or a training class, visit several before you decide which one is for you; watch their methods, and talk to the trainer about how they expect your puppy to progress. If you are hoping to take part in any of the disciplines it is still not necessary to participate when your puppy is young; as much as it may be fun for you, it is still an extra learning curve usually outside the canine instinct that he will be learning. However, if you talk to the trainer they will be able to guide you in certain areas as to how your dog will be expected to walk, sit, stay, and so on, depending on what discipline you have chosen, enabling you to do some preparation training at home. Also if you visit local clubs you may find a trainer who provides puppy training in a manner that will encourage obedience and good manners.

What If?

My Puppy does not like Crowds

There is a reason for everything, so first of all ask yourself why he is nervous of people, and don't jump to conclusions without exploring all the possibilities. We humans are good at selecting obvious reasons rather than doing more research, but if we don't find the reason for the problem, then we cannot proceed down the correct avenue to rectify it. There are likely to be two main reasons for the puppy's behaviour: it has been made nervous by a person or persons, and it has not had the support or protection of a pack leader or a senior canine. The claims of 'it happened when someone else had been looking after it – because it wasn't socialized – it was over-socialized – the vet did it – it was too young – too old' or any other of these, still throw the onus back on the owner. For if any, all, or another reason caused the puppy's distrust of other people, how did the owner come to allow it to happen? It is possible a puppy can be genetically nervous, but as discussed in a previous chapter, a nervous puppy can be encouraged to be bold by a sympathetic pack leader.

The answer is not to take your puppy into crowded areas or anywhere that will cause him distress. He is telling you he does not feel safe, but his lack of confidence is in his pack leader, thus leading to the fear of others; so if you continue to take him into the situation that you know causes him concern, he will eventually lose faith in you altogether. Go back to basics, regain his confidence in you at home, and ask yourself how it can have gone wrong: Has he been pulling on a lead, walking in front, not coming back when called? Have you been a good friend but not a very safe leader? Have you taken him to a crowded area or allowed someone in his space that he did not welcome? If someone else has let him down, then you gave them permission to do so, therefore you are the one who needs to build bridges to regain his confidence. Once his faith in you is restored, he will trust you to look after him. Not all dogs like crowded areas, not all dogs welcome the attention of people, and a dog cannot be blamed for its characteristics and genetical make-up; and if we try to change them, we are usually the losers. Understand your dog, know his strengths and weaknesses, and learn to live with them.

My Puppy does not like Children

If the children your puppy is objecting to are yours, what have they been doing to make him resent them? Children of all ages should be taught how to look after a puppy or an older dog, and they should be encouraged to participate in the training. Back to the drawing board again, but on this occasion it is the children that have to be re-educated, and the puppy's confidence must be restored in them as well as in you. If your puppy does not like children in general, it is possible he has been frightened by a child; small children can appear very threatening to a puppy, they smell strange, they walk in a different way to older children and adults, and their faces are very near eye contact with the puppy. Or maybe he is just not used to children and therefore he has a natural wariness of them. I never encourage or welcome strangers to stroke my dogs without my permission, and I always make sure that children keep a distance until I have a chance to introduce them properly. My dogs are quite comfortable around children, and some of them are used in remedial work for children with confidence problems; however, they have never been subjected to unwelcome advances, therefore they have no reason to be suspicious or nervous. Quite often a young dog that is unsure of children will change and become a child-friendly adult dog if it is left alone by children and the owner allows the dog to mature a little. Many adult human beings are confident in situations that they were nervous of when young and unsure of themselves. Confidence has to be nurtured, encouraged and allowed to develop, it does not happen overnight.

My Puppy has started Nipping

What makes it think it can nip? What makes it think it can make the decision to use its teeth? Why is it using its teeth at all? The first few chapters of this book explain what makes a puppy think it has the right to use its teeth. The sad part about any puppy nipping, biting or being destructive is that it will not be doing anything wrong, because in its eyes, it thinks it has been given permission to do so – in fact if it could talk, it would probably say it had been *encouraged* to do so. First check the energy you are feeding, then all toys, balls and anything that he is used to chewing must be put away. Leave him with a bone or similar to chew, and provide him with a place to chew it.

Begin an 'in-house' training programme by monitoring his behaviour and his manners in your home. Does he rush around everywhere, does he run in front at doors, does he regard you, or does he ignore you? Have you played tuggy games with him, and have you encouraged him to chew or tug leads, sleeves, toys? Begin to

rebuild the foundation of good manners, make it quite clear to him who is the leader and that concessions must be earned. If this is a very young puppy, then one day of re-education should bring him back into your pack as a respectable youngster. But if he is older you will have to be more astute with your observations as to why and how it happened, for you are not re-educating a baby – you will have the beginnings of a wayward youngster on your hands.

I Already have Another Dog

If you have an older dog when you get your puppy, you will have to make sure that you do not push the older one out, as this can cause jealousy. However, I do not believe you should resort to proving to the younger one that there should be a 'pecking order' when it comes to feeding, grooming, attention, games, walks and so on. You do not have to provide a 'pecking order' because you are the pack leader and your decision is final, so if you decided to make them

It may seem harmless when a puppy wants to play with an older dog, but the older dog must be completely trustworthy, and the two must never be left unattended.

A puppy playfully nipping the mouth as it would with its mother and siblings, but the big dog could seriously harm him with just one push of his body.

This young chap looks stocky and as if he could cope with anything . . .

. . . but he is still a puppy, and he is not sure how to handle this situation with the older dogs. He would like the stick, but if he goes to get it the other dogs could hurt him or damage his joints without intending to, just by engaging in gentle play fighting.

both eat out of the same bowl then they must accept your decision and live with it. However, there is such a thing as respect for a senior canine (far better words than 'pecking order'), and no dog should be subjected to endless pestering from a youngster; furthermore they should both be able to eat in privacy, as should dogs of any age. Toys should not be provided *ad lib* as they can cause arguments; each one should have one toy of their own, and you should not encourage interchanging. Yes, many dogs do swap toys, and equally just as many puppies have suffered severe bites from senior canines who were left to sort out problems because the pack leader (the dogs' owners) did not make provision for separate private areas and toys for them.

Be very careful that your puppy does not emulate your older dog all the time, in particular pick up any bad habits it has, and identify with it as its pack leader – if this happens it will leave you far down the line of importance. Spend time with them separately, exercise them separately whenever you can, and bring them up as two individuals; if you do not, they may form a partnership you cannot control.

Do not allow your older dog to play rough-and-tumble games with your puppy; whether it is the same breed, a smaller breed or a larger one, a great deal of damage can be done to a puppy's joints and back by incorrect handling. Few dogs have the ability to play with a puppy in the manner they would in the wild, and if they have been brought up to play games with balls and toys and to chase, they will use the puppy as a surrogate toy. All interaction must be gentle, and you must make sure you are there to intervene and, if possible, to teach the older dog how to play without chasing and running.

I Want to Get Another Dog

If you are wanting to bring another dog into your family I strongly advise waiting until you have built up a good relationship with your puppy, until it is well mannered, and you are sure there are no problems looming on the horizon that need taking care of first. In my opinion a puppy deserves at least one year with you before you introduce another dog. For the reasons I have already given – such as rough playing and jealousy – you could end up with serious behavioural problems. You need to be able to spend quality time with your puppy, it deserves it, but so does any other dog you have. So to bring in a newcomer when the first still needs time and attention means that someone may go short of that all-important quality time of just you and your dog bonding and learning together.

I Want to Get Two Puppies

I have no hesitation in advising anyone who wants to buy two puppies together to say, 'No, don't do it'. It doesn't matter if they are of the same litter, different litters or if they are of totally different breeds, the answer is the same. You are taking into your home two small beings, they will both recognize certain instincts in each other, and even if they are different breeds, they are still canines. They will converse with each other, play with each other, learn about pack instincts together, and they will form a bond that can leave you standing on the outside of their very private little 'puppy club'. This is not why you are getting a puppy: you want it to converse with *you*, to share things with *you*, to form a bond with *you*. If you have two puppies, neither one of them will get the quality time with you that would have been prevalent had there been only one: however much you try you will always be sharing your time and your attentions. It is not impossible, and I have known people who have brought up two puppies and they have a good relationship with them, but it is on a joint basis and not an individual one.

I have also done many consultations for people who are just a 'hanger-on' in their pack of two dogs which they have had from puppies and that have taken over. When bringing up two together is successful, it is with an experienced dog handler used to bringing up puppies – but even then there is always an 'if I'd only had one we would have shared more together'. I have done it myself when I have had no choice, and I have always been conscious that each dog had to 'share' me during their most important formative years. No matter how good you are, you cannot split yourself in two, or make each hour repeat itself.

My Puppy is Possessive

If he is possessive of toys, then I fear he is probably suffering from the 'too many, too soon' syndrome – in which case the answer is simple: remove them until your puppy appreciates that everything belongs to you and concessions must be earned. If your puppy is possessive of food, has it always been like this, or has it developed gradually? Puppies are usually fed together in a group when they are first weaned, so it is possible yours has had to defend his meals from his brothers and sisters. If this is the case he will benefit from being fed in a quiet place and left to eat in peace until he realizes that his food is not likely to be stolen. However, if it has developed grad-

ually, you will have to ask yourself when it started and what could have caused it. Has he been teased, has another dog tried to take it from him, is he hungry, have you provided him with a quiet dining area? Don't keep trying to take it from him, because by trying to prove a point you could make him worse. Ignore any demands to feed him before you are ready, make him sit and wait before you give it to him, and then leave him to eat it. You must not be dictated to by him, you will feed him when and where you want, but then he deserves to be left to eat in peace. Once he realizes he is not getting special attention from you, and that his food is not under threat, there is little point in him wasting his energy trying to be possessive over it.

If your puppy is possessive of a person, usually the owner, then he is seeing himself as being in control. It is not his place to protect you unless you have given him permission to do so, and quite often a little show of possessiveness is flattering, but if it goes uncorrected your puppy will think this is expected of him, especially if the first time gained him some attention.

Teaching your Pack Area on a Walk

You have taught your puppy all about your pack area where you live and you have provided mental and physical boundaries for him to live by. You have taught him the importance of good manners, he has his own 'bed', somewhere to play, dig, and enjoy a quiet moment on his own. When you go for a walk he knows to respect you as his pack leader, and to wait and see where you are going to take him, and at what speed. He knows to stop and to wait, and to come back when called when he hears whatever instructions you have chosen to use. He is confident that you will look after him and protect him, and this makes him a confident little chap in company; however he knows not to be demanding. He also knows to wait his turn, and to give way to senior pack members. But what happens when you let him off the lead where there are no fences or walls, just acres of land and lots of lovely smells?

It could be a temptation for your puppy to throw respect out of the window, to run away and only come back when he is ready, and not give a button about you shouting and pleading with him to come back. It could happen, but it won't. Why should it, he wants to be with you, he knows you will let him sniff all the wonderful things on offer when the time is right for him to do so, and he is content to do what you say because you are wonderful. Dogs do like to run and they do like to sniff, but they cannot leave the pack area and they cannot dictate what, where and when. If they are not prepared to stop, turn round, and come back to you when you say, then they cannot go in the first place. Concessions must be earned.

Puppies are not allowed to wander away from mum, and when they join the main pack they must stay within the 'safety net' of the senior canines. If they stray and keep straying further and further outside the pack perimeter, the pack leader will tell them off, for as they mature they will become a renegade pack running along-side his, making their own decisions and trying to take over from him. If he allows this to happen he has shown a weakness, and will therefore lose the respect of the pack. A good mum will have taught them not to go over the boundary, and a good pack leader will stop them before they get there. Puppies that stray risk the security of the rest of the pack, so this lesson in pack boundaries is learned quickly; besides an instinctive knowledge of the boundary rule will be in most dogs,

Three little puppies learning to walk behind.

waiting to be respected or ignored. You will notice in the first few days that he will only ever be a certain distance from you: this is the distance he deems to be safe, the distance where if anything untoward happens you, as his protector, are within easy reach. When you have discovered this distance, instead of letting him reach the perimeter and deciding himself that he is nearing the edge of the safety zone, it is up to you to tell him, 'This is your boundary'. Each time he nears the distance where he would look back at you, introduce him to a new instruction, such as 'enough', or 'far enough', or anything else you can relate to and feel comfortable using. In time he will think it is you designating the pack boundary and not him showing you where it is. Never wait until he has reached the boundary, but always tell him before he gets there that he is not allowed to go any further.

You can practise this in the house and in the garden. When you first go out for a walk and he is anxious to be near you, use the boundary command. Wherever you are, and whatever age he is, the boundary is never more than twenty-five yards away from you, and it is in a circle all around you. So in theory you have an imaginary circle around you and it goes wherever you are, you are always in the centre of it and your puppy never leaves it. When he is behind you in his own space he must still stay within the circle, so no hanging back on a walk. When you give him permission to enter your space and to walk in front of you, he must still stay within the circle. And if you have an imaginary circle of twenty-five yards and your puppy begins to ignore you at twenty yards, then you must reduce the size of your circle to eighteen yards. The sizes are all approximate: what is important is that *you* always

dictate the perimeter, not him. When your puppy does everything you ask of him within the circle – he recalls first time, every time, and he is always listening to you – give him permission to go a few yards outside the circle if he wants to. If he is happy to stay within the circle, don't try to make him leave it: the more he wants to be with you, the less he will want to be far away. This may mean that you have to walk further to exercise him if you cannot just let him run off and do as he pleases, but having a dog is about walking and spending time together. There is

Two little puppies striding out. Ben and Pip have learned about the four non-negotiable commands, they know about staying within the pack area, and on a walk they will stay behind until invited to come to the side.

absolutely no reason why a dog should be two, three or four hundred yards away from its owner – it is on its own, making its own decisions, and then it can be a danger, or be in danger.

The Ideal Relationship

We accept our children for who they are, we can have hopes and dreams for them, but as individuals they have a right to choose whether to follow our dreams or realize ones of their own. Your dog has little choice but to help you try and realize any dreams you have for him. You may imagine competing, jogging or swimming together – but if he really does not like water he cannot swim, if he is not athletic or suffers from any health defect, jogging and competing will remain just dreams. Does it matter? He is a living being, and these were not his dreams, they were

yours, and even if he cannot help you realize them, he can still be a faithful, loyal, lovable companion to you.

If he is capable of doing all the things you ever dreamed of doing together, don't rush him. No young dog should be going over jumps, however small, running endlessly after balls, or be engaged in the sharp twisting and turning that is often part of energetic ball games; he needs to develop, and his muscles, tendons, bones and joints need to be strong enough to be able to cope with all the demands that such games can put on his body. If a dog is still growing at six months his body is not ready to produce great gymnastic feats, and when his growth rate slows down he is still not ready. Only when he has stopped growing and has filled out can the demands on his body be turned to the things you are waiting to do with him. This means that you are not going to be spending time preparing for a hectic

No puppy should do excessive running, twisting and turning, and jumping of any height should be postponed until the puppy is a fully developed dog. Too much, too soon can result in a dog with joint and hip problems later. This dog is fully developed, but is still only allowed to do small jumps.

And then there was one. Ben is a confident, happy puppy. He has no fear of people, and will go to anyone when given permission to do so. He is not frightened of other dogs, but he does not approach strange dogs. He is not an angel, he is a normal, happy little chap who likes to test the boundaries. He no longer needs Mossie to look after him, but he does like to spend some time with her. He is the grandson of my daughter's first dog Lass, and the special relationship she and Lass shared is already there in this cheeky little lad. The loyalty in Ben is in every puppy, it just needs nurturing.

future until his body is ready, so it means patience – but this patience will be rewarded by the empathy you are creating with one another.

Teaching him his name will not be difficult, as he will hear it often enough to learn to respond when he hears it; but try to resist the temptation to use it each time you give him an instruction. If you are constantly using his name – Fido come, Fido sit – you are undermining the importance of the instruction; he will also not respond to his name when you are trying to gain his attention, as he will have heard it so often that he will not give it any reverence.

This puppy is yours, you have probably waited a long time for him, and the excitement of actually having him in your home on that very first day is wonderful. But always take time to stop and 'think dog', make sure you always consider his feelings, and try to see the world as he sees it. There is a subtle difference between your puppy dictating what he wants, and you considering what he needs. If he demands your attention don't be told what to do, but make him sit and wait and then invite him to you for attention. But if he has been good for a length of time and just wants to be with you, then he is not demanding, he is loving. We can decipher different attitudes, moods and feelings in members of our family because we study them, we understand them, and we make the effort to be patient when necessary. All it takes to create an empathy with your puppy is time, patience and the willingness to see and understand his point of view.

A partnership is built on trust and respect, it is knowing what the other needs without having to ask, of being content with each other's company without the need for words. You can create this with your puppy, because there is nothing a dog wants more than to have someone to be loyal to, it is in their very soul to give without question and always to be there for you. It is not hard to return this compliment, it just takes a little patience and understanding; but the benefits you reap will far outweigh any accolades you may receive later. He will always be there when you need him, he will not demand explanations, and he will never turn his back on you. If you work hard at trying to understand him he will try equally hard to understand you. When he is a sensible adult dog and the two of you are sharing a quiet moment together whilst on a walk, you can look at him and be proud of all you have achieved.

INDEX